Belvidere Republican

Belvidere Illlustrated

Historical, Descriptive and Biographical

Belvidere Republican

Belvidere Illustrated
Historical, Descriptive and Biographical

ISBN/EAN: 9783337014162

Printed in Europe, USA, Canada, Australia, Japan

Cover: Foto ©ninafisch / pixelio.de

More available books at **www.hansebooks.com**

HISTORICAL, DESCRIPTIVE AND BIOGRAPHICAL

PRICE, ONE DOLLAR AND FIFTY CENTS

BELVIDERE, ILL.
PUBLISHED BY THE DAILY REPUBLICAN
1896

DEDICATED

TO THE INTERESTS OF BELVIDERE, THE CITY OF SEWING MACHINES AND BICYCLES.

THE BEST CITY OF ITS SIZE IN THE STATE.

BELVIDERE ILLUSTRATED.

Standing on the threshold of the year of our Lord, eighteen hundred and ninety-six, the enterprising city of Belvidere is looking into a future which seems to be fraught with a healthy prosperity, and pregnant with the brightest possibilities.

Few cities in the United States passed through the disastrous panic of 1893 in a condition as free from financial depression as Belvidere. Despite the univer-

STATE STREET, LOOKING NORTH FROM GEN. FULLER'S OFFICE.
PHOTO BY CLARK & NOTT.

sal stagnation the city marched proudly on in its progress, until now it has attained a momentum which bids fair to give us an additional population of five thousand within the next ten years.

Belvidere in 1896. These few words briefly indicate the purpose kept in view in preparing and issuing this souvenir edition of THE REPUBLICAN — to picture Belvidere as it is to-day.

Belvidere is known as one of the most beautiful small cities in the state of Illinois, and as an attractive and most desirable place of residence, blessed with superior educational, religious and social advantages. The products of its manufactories have made an enviable reputation in commercial circles throughout the country, and its business enterprises, interests and relations are constantly extending and increasing in importance.

The pages which follow invite the attention of the reader to the manifold attractions offered by Belvidere as a beautiful and desirable place of residence, to the inexhaustible supply of cheap fuel easily obtainable, to the advantages it possesses as a manufacturing center, to the unsurpassed richness and fertility of the agricultural region tributary to the city, to its transportation facilities, to the importance of its sewing-machine and bicycle manufactory, to the progressive spirit

COURT HOUSE.

exhibited by the people, and to the substantial foundations upon which its past prosperity has rested, and which point unerringly to its more rapid progress and advancement as each coming year shall roll by.

In presenting this beautiful souvenir to the public THE REPUBLICAN recognizes the fact that it is in some respects imperfect, that some points have perhaps been overlooked, and that it fails to do complete justice to all the varied advantages and attractions of Belvidere, but THE REPUBLICAN has spared neither labor nor expense in the effort to present as accurately and completely as possible the Belvidere of to-day, and is confident that no publication ever issued has pictured our city as accurately, as completely, and as attractively. Nor has any publication as elaborate and as expensive ever been undertaken in any city no larger than this, and the mere fact that an undertaking of such magnitude has been successfully carried out in Belvidere demonstrates the truth of all that is said in these pages in regard to the public spirit, enterprise and liberality of its citizens, and the importance of its business interests. From the inception of this enterprise THE REPUBLICAN has received the hearty encouragement and cordial support of the enterprising business men and public spirited citizens of Belvidere, and takes pleasure in acknowledging their active co-operation, and in saying that to them the gratifying success of this publication is principally due.

BELVIDERE IN EARLY DAYS.

Picturesquely located on the banks of the Kishwaukee river, in Boone County, seventy-five miles west from Chicago, and occupying the slopes of gently retreating elevations, the Belvidere of to-day, with its eight thousand inhabitants, invites

BUSINESS PORTION OF NORTH STATE STREET.

comparison and tempts to citizenship. Its history makes record of sixty years, but its real progressive life began with the advent of manufactories ten years ago.

In 1835 the first comers encamped beside the stream, on whose borders, near the present fair-grounds, was at the time assembled a band of Pottawattomie Indians, which in a few months removed beyond the Mississippi. Their council-house, nearly in ruins, and the remains of the chieftain, Big Thunder, within a paling enclosure on the Mound, for a brief period gave evidence of former occupation.

The earliest settlers in this vicinity were Archibald Metcalf, David Dunham, John K. Towner, Cornelius Cline, Erastus A. Nixon, S. P. Doty and Dr. D. H. Whitney. Messrs. Cline, Nixon and Towner made their first pilgrimage from Chicago on foot, returning for their families. Mrs. Towner was the first white woman to tread the soil of Belvidere. This section was mainly peopled by emigrants from the New England and Middle states, and their sturdy type has given character to the population of later years.

In August, 1835, Ebenezer Peck and Dr. Goodhue came out from Chicago on a prospecting tour, and, admiring the situation, purchased, with Nathaniel Crosby, Dunham and Metcalf's claim, which included the present site of North Belvidere. Its name was changed to that now designating the city in honor of Mr. Peck's native place in Canada. The "Belvidere Company" was shortly after organized, with a capital stock of $10,000, for the purpose of building saw and grist mills and developing the property. John S. King, Jacob Whitman, J. C. Goodhue, S. P. Doty, F. W. Crosby, J. P. Chapin, Joel Parker and H. L. Crosby were admitted to partnership with the original purchasers of the claim. Soon after the mills

SOUTH BELVIDERE SCHOOL, NO. 1.

were erected and the land placed on the market. In October a census gave Belvidere a population of thirty-seven men, women and children.

In June, 1836, the state road was located, with Belvidere on the route. August 1st of this year the first election was held in Belvidere precinct, at which thirty-seven persons voted. Some time in the fall of 1836 the town site was laid off into lots, and the corners of State and Mechanic streets (the latter now Lincoln avenue) determined by a carpenter's square. On these four corners were the business houses from 1836 to 1840. The building now on the southwest corner was the first brick structure erected in Belvidere. In December, 1836, a postoffice was established, it being the first on the northern stage route from Chicago to Galena. S. S. Whitman was appointed postmaster.

May 3, 1837, was held the first county election. In 1838 bids for a courthouse were solicited, but not until 1843 was the building completed. Its cost was $6,000. Its successor, the present court-house, was finished Sept. 12, 1855, after an expenditure of $10,000. Later the record building was erected, and the county and circuit clerk's offices removed thereto. In the year 1838 political lines were first drawn between adherents of the Whig and Democratic parties.

:EARLY ORGANIZATION.

In 1847 Belvidere was organized as a town, in conformity to the general state law, but for various reasons remained under its operation only one year. In March, 1857, it incorporated as a town, with a special charter, and elected its first Board of five Trustees—J. K. Towner, Israel Tripp, D. W. Read, Cephas Gardner and Warren Pierce. The latter was selected as president, which position fell to one of the number, *ex-officio*. During the intervening ten years the town's affairs were administered by the county judge and two associate justices.

The first bridge was thrown across the river at what is now State street in 1837. Prior to that time the crossing had been at fords, the principal one being at Main street. Here Scott's army passed over in 1832.

SOUTH BELVIDERE SCHOOL, NO. 2.
PHOTO BY CLARK & NOTT.

In 1852 came the railroad, elsewhere referred to. The next decade witnessed a marvelous development. Prior to this year the possibility of extending the town to the south side of the river had been under consideration, and the location of the railroad made the step practicable. The building of warehouses and stores began, and in time the center of trade gravitated to the new division, with a resulting increase of population which now gives it a preponderance in comparison with that of the city generally.

OUR PART IN THE WAR.

The record of Belvidere in connection with the war of the rebellion, with that of the whole county, is one which will be scanned with pride by coming generations. Over two thousand men were sent into the field. Many of them attained to distinction in military and civic service, and the names of Fuller, Hurlbut, Humphrey, Loop, Bush, Haywood, Baker, with scores of others, will live in the annals of those eventful years. During the war the county appropriated $161,000 for bounties and aid to soldiers' families. In addition, the separate towns appro-

FIRST METHODIST CHURCH.
PHOTO BY CLARK & NOTT.

priated $92,000, of which Belvidere's proportion was $38,000; and to be added to this is the sum of $63,000, voluntarily contributed, making a total of $315,000 disbursed for the soldiers and their loved ones at home. Every appeal for men and means found prompt response, and the great heart of the people went out to the brave boys at the front.

BANKS OF BELVIDERE.

The banking facilities have always been fully adequate. Among the first established institutions were the Boone County Bank and the Belvidere Bank. The latter, whose president was Alexander Neely, went into liquidation many years ago. The former, owned by Fuller, Lawrence & Company, was converted into the First National in 1865. At various dates other banks flourished for limited periods, in the list being those operated by Yourt, Lawrence & Company, M. G. Leonard and W. H. Gilman. The banks now furnishing accommoda-

REV. WM. CRAVEN.

tion are the First National, Second National and People's (State). The officers of the First National are: Mark Ramsey, president; William S. Dunton, vice-president; A. E. Loop, cashier; Charles D. Loop, assistant cashier. Its resources are: Loans and discounts, $92,301.47; stocks, bonds and securities, $124,490.60; other items, $33,120.14; total, $249,912.21. The liabilities are: Capital stock, $75,000; surplus fund and undivided profits, $21,767.94; National bank notes outstanding, $22,500; deposits, $130,644.27. The Second National has for officers: Allen C. Fuller, president; D. D. Sabin, vice-president; Irving Terwilliger, cashier; Frank Sewell, assistant cashier. Its resources are: Loans and discounts, $137,438.98; stocks and securities, $126,940; other items, $91,312.65; total, $355,691.63. The liabilities are: Capital stock, $100,000; deposits, $201,574.31; surplus fund and

NORTH BELVIDERE SCHOOL.
PHOTO BY CLARK & NOTT.

undivided profits, $32,101.11; other items, $22,016.21. The People's Bank is officered as follows: W. D. Swail, president; F. S. Whitman, vice-president; John Greenlee, cashier; B. F. Harnish, assistant cashier; William Greenlee, second assistant cashier. Its resources are: Loans and discounts, $183,923.55; bonds, $55,550.88; other items, $59,732.85; total, $299,207.28. The liabilities are: Capital stock, $50,000; deposits, $227,458.71; surplus fund and undivided profits, $21,748.57.

WE BECOME A CITY.

Belvidere was incorporated as a city in 1882, and divided into four wards. In May of that year its first officers were elected. The first mayor was W. D. Swail, and those succeeding were: F. S. Whitman, John Hannah, George H. Hurlbut, and the present incumbent. The city officials now are: Dr. R. W. McInnis, mayor; A. E. Jenner, city clerk; R. W. Wright, corporation counsel; F. J.

PRESBYTERIAN CHURCH.
PHOTO BY W. H. ROBINSON.

Evans, city attorney; J. H. Cook, treasurer; L. E. Benson, street commissioner; George H. Hurlbut, engineer; E. E. Spooner, superintendent waterworks; William Richardson, chief of police; John Thren, fire marshal; board of aldermen: first ward, A. W. Robinson, F. H. Dixon; second ward, A. A. Slafter, J. W. Sharp; third ward, B. B. McFall, P. R. Kennedy; fourth ward, F. W. Crain, W. H. Moore. The board of health is composed of Mayor McInnis, Dr. A. W. Swift, Dr. Willis Butterfield, and the city marshal.

An ordinance, approved January 25, 1896, appropriated the following amounts for the purposes indicated: Sinking fund, $11,500; interest fund, $632.50; salary of officers, $1,305; miscellaneous expenses, $750; city engineering department, $300; police department, $3,530; street lighting, $3,900; legal expenses, $450; health department, $150; fire department, $3,775; waterworks, $12,912.71; general street work, $4,260; library fund, $700; total, $44,165.21. The expenditures during 1895 were $42,700.32, but of this sum a certain proportion was for obligations of the previous year. That this

REV. GEO. R. PIERCE, D. D.

amount has been wisely expended is attested by the condition of the streets and various public improvements, and the service rendered by the different departments. The population of the city, according to the last school census, was 8,000.

A SANITARY SEWER SYSTEM.

The pressing need of an effective sewerage system became so apparent that last year the council passed an ordinance providing for a survey and estimate with reference to initial work. This was undertaken and completed by J. W. Alvord, a Chicago hydraulic engineer. The portion of the city to be provided for includes the principal business streets and such connecting thoroughfares as it will be possible to cover at present. The system will be gradually extended until every section of the city is reached.

PERIOD OF GROWTH.

From the close of the war until the inauguration of manufacturing, the experience of Belvidere was that of other communities depending entirely upon the rural districts for revenue. It, however, prospered, but the increase of population was moderate, and its resources, while available to the amount necessary for ordinary purposes, permitted little in the way of public improvements. With the transfer from Chicago of the June plant, eventually the National Sewing Machine Company, now one of the most important representatives of this industry in the whole country, began the wonderful advancement of the city. Other corporations followed the initial company, and more are to avail themselves of the superior advantages offered by this central and promising location. The new elements infused life, the growth in numbers and increase of means warranted the undertaking of larger enterprises, and its recent past gives promise of a prosperous future to the individual and the municipality.

OUR PUBLIC LIBRARY.

The Ida Public Library originated from a donation of $5,000 by General Fuller in 1883, and is located in the city hall building. It has for officers: President, Allen C. Fuller; Vice President, W. D. Swail; Secretary, Irving Terwilliger; Librarian, Miss Mary F. Crandall; Asst. Librarian, Miss Nellie Greenlee. Its board of directors is composed of the three officers first named, with the addition of Messrs. A. C. Fassett and J. C. Foote, and Mesdames G. H. Hurlbut, E. T. Gage, J. R. Balliet and C. E. Scott. The number of books is 9,650, with circulation for the year 1894-5 of 23,950. The last register number of cards issued is 2,708.

REV. F. C. STIERLE.
PHOTO BY CLARK & NOTT.

FACTS ABOUT OUR CITY.

The city hall, a fine structure centrally located, was erected in 1884, at an expense of $10,000. On the main floor is the postoffice and in the second story are the council chamber, city clerk's office and the Ida public library.

On September 6 of last year John M. Roach, of Chicago, was granted permission by ordinance to build and operate an electric railway on various principal streets. The road was incorporated and has a capital stock of $35,000. The intention is to complete the line during the present year.

The present plan of street lighting, by arc lamps suspended at street intersections, was adopted in 1887. The service now is sixty lights, at an annual expense of $3,900.

Two telephone exchanges, the Central Union and Belvidere, using four hundred phones, give Belvidere plenty of chance to talk.

The volunteer fire department, which has always rendered the best service possible under existing conditions, was superseded during the present year by a paid department, with horses and wagons and a complete equipment.

Free postal delivery was commenced April 1, Belvidere being the only city in the state this year securing the privilege. One desirable result of this concession by the postoffice department is the proper numbering of every building, it being made compulsory.

WATER WORKS BUILDING.
PHOTO BY CLARK & NOTT.

REV. J. A. PIERCE.

SOUTH BAPTIST CHURCH.

Belvidere is noted among other things for the unusually high character of its people. It represents the most valued elements of older communities, and is an illustration of development under the refining influences of the best social and intellectual life.

To the business men of Belvidere must be accredited, in the main, the advancement of the city. They were quick to apprehend the situation and improve it. Their hearty co-operation in all projects looking to the forwarding of the city's interests made them possible of realization. With general prosperity came modern methods of handling trade. New buildings for store purposes, equipped with all desirable conveniences, and filled with more extensive and varied stocks,

THE CITY HALL AND POST-OFFICE.

VIEW OF MILK CONDENSING FACTORY FROM RAILROAD BRIDGE.
PHOTO BY CLARK & NOTT.

adapted to the improved demand, have replaced nearly all the older inferior structures. In sound condition, and transacting a large business, the merchants of Belvidere are reaping the harvest of wise preparation.

The advantages offered to manufacturers are in many respects exceptional. The admirable railroad facilities, central locations available, disposition of the people to afford every facility, the desirability of the city for residence—combine to present attractions that should lead to numerous accessions.

ST. JAMES CATHOLIC CHURCH.
PHOTO BY CLARK & NOTT.

In no other city of its size are greater generosity or more perfect union, with reference to the undertaking of public or industrial enterprises, exhibited by its business men and capitalists. With a purpose to extend the hand of fellowship to intending citizens, to promote and foster every worthy essay of a business and general nature, and to carry forward the extensive system of public improvements already well inaugurated—Belvidere confidently offers inducements superior to those of any other among the smaller cities of the west.

What has been said with regard to the progress of and inducements held out by Belvidere is not by any means in the line of exaggeration. Its business, conveniences, improvements, facilities and privileges are in evidence, and substantiate the statements made. With many of the belongings of metropolitan existence—among them a perfect water supply, telephone exchanges, electric and gas lighting and heating, and in the immediate future a complete sewerage system, street railways, effective fire department service, street paving, and free postal delivery—the material comfort of its people will be well provided for, while its higher advantages will meet the requirement of every acquisition.

The "Belvidere of To-Day," though flourishing and attractive, is yet but an

A GEM OF NATURE SEEN AT KELLEY'S ISLAND.
PHOTO BY CLARK & NOTT.

index of the "Coming Belvidere," made possible by its situation and resources, and the energy and purpose of its people.

MANY BEAUTIFUL HOMES.

Within the last ten years a complete transformation has been effected in the residence districts of the city. The first move in the direction of modern construction was a revelation, and duplication speedily followed. Thenceforward the spirit of friendly emulation appeared to take possession of the people, and structures vieing in elegance and costliness with those adorning more pretentious centers, together with many of lesser value but architectural beauty, were placed in every

THE DAM BELOW THE CITY.
PHOTO BY GUY ALLEN.

quarter of the city. The prevailing ideas were also applied to the older dwellings, and their remodeling accompanied the erection of newer buildings. In the numerous additions, also, required by the growing city, this combination of utility with artistic finish was steadily kept in view. The grounds about these lovely homes are in keeping, and ornamented with shrubbery and shade trees in the profusion which space will still allow. The trees upon the different residence thoroughfares have been wisely protected and their planting encouraged, and in summer days the shadows of the street rival those of the forest road. The erection of handsome and expensive blocks, and adapting of structures of earlier dates to modern requirements have entirely changed the appearance of the business streets. The

BELVIDERE CEMETERY.
PHOTO BY W. H. ROBINSON.

drives about the city, the charming views, its spacious parks, the evidences of taste and refinement on every hand, substantiate the claim of Belvidere to be an exceptionally beautiful and desirable place of residence.

WATERWORKS.

The agitation for a better water-supply culminated during the year 1889 in the purchase of a site on which are located the present artesian well and pumping station. The work of drilling immediately began, and a well 1,950 feet in depth, with a diameter of eight inches for 1,200 feet and six inches for the balance of the distance, resulted. An abundant flow of water in purest quality was secured. The mayor was John Hannah, and the aldermen: John C. Starr, O. H. Wright, Jr., W. H. Derthick, R. H. Jukes, R. F. Tousley, F. R. Smiley, G. H. Hurlbut, E. A. Cleaveland. Messrs. Smiley, Jukes and Tousley composed the fire and water committee. Mr. E. E. Spooner was summoned from Rochelle, Ill., to superintend its construction. The necessary buildings and standpipe were at once erected, machinery purchased, and mains extended over a wide area. The total of mains laid amounts to 10½ miles; number of hydrants set, 99; number of valves, 43; number of services, 475.

At the well are: The basin, holding 80,000 gallons, and the station house, in which are three engines — one triplex, one compound and one double extension, the two latter having a daily energy of 1,000,000 gallons each. The standpipe, located on the Mound, half a mile from the station, has a capacity of 42,000 gallons, and its apex is 173 feet above datum. The mains are 4, 6, 8 and 10 inches in diameter. A second standpipe is being erected.

The ordinary pressure is 60 to 70 pounds, but for fires 120 pounds, although in the latter instance frequently exceeding this register. The capacity of the well is about 700,000 gallons each twenty-four hours. The largest amount consumed in any one day was during the last summer, when it reached 401,000. In the month of August last 8,016,435 gallons were sent through the mains. In January of this year the figure was 3,778,740. The average delivery is

GERMAN LUTHERAN CHURCH.
PHOTO BY CLARK & SOTT.

REV. E. HEINEMANN.
PHOTO BY YOUNDT.

about 300,000 gallons daily in summer, and 135,000 in winter.

Appropriations have been made for an additional water-tower, with connections, to be placed near the junction of Pearl and Fifth streets, in the south division, at an expense of $8,000. This will have a capacity of 128,000 gallons, or nearly three times that of the present tower.

CHURCHES OF BELVIDERE.

Among the inquiries of intending emigrants to the West, whose relations with church organizations in their Eastern homes were about to terminate, those regarding the religious privileges possible of enjoyment

FIRST BAPTIST CHURCH.
PHOTO BY W. H. ROBINSON.

in the newer country had precedence.

Very early in the history of Belvidere could be transmitted the intelligence that societies had been formed, under permanent leadership, and in the succeeding years reports of encouraging growth. With the increase of population all leading denominations found representation, and at the first opportunity houses of worship were erected. The humble structures originally serving as places of convocation were supplanted, as means accumulated, by elegant and costly edifices.

This may truthfully be termed a church-going people. Within the walls of its sanctuaries are gathered the best representatives of the city's social and business life. To the churches of Belvidere, as of other communities, must be awarded the larger share of credit for its moral and intellectual as well as material advancement. There follow sketches of the different organizations, so far as data has been available.

METHODIST CHURCH.

Some time during the year 1838 the first Methodist preacher was heard in Belvidere. In 1850 the brick church on the North Side was built. In 1866 about twenty-four of the members of the First Church on the North Side withdrew and formed a Class on the South Side. Until 1876 regular preaching services were held in both churches. In that year the Rev. N. H. Axtell supplied the two societies. The same arrangement was continued

REV. R. S. WALKER.

under the pastorate of Rev. W. S. Harrington. In 1879 Rev. O. E. Burch was appointed to the First Church, and the Rev. G. C. Clark to the Church on the South Side. The two churches were occupied until 1885 when under the pastorate of Rev. S. H. Swartz the two societies united, and have so continued until the present. During the pastorates of Revs. Cessna, Bigelow and Craven a new church edifice was planned and completed, and dedicated by the Rev. Lewis Curts, of Chicago, Feb. 12, 1893. The church is a splendid modern building, seating in the main auditorium 675, and with the lecture-room 925. The church, pipe organ costing $2,500, and parsonage are worth $25,000. The membership has increased to 507, and the Sunday School has 350 names enrolled, with an average attendance of 250. Few

IMMANUEL EPISCOPAL CHURCH.
PHOTO BY CLARK & NOTT.

churches are so well equipped for worship. Its officers are: Rev. S. M. Merrill, D. D., resident bishop; Rev. F. A. Hardin, D. D., presiding elder; Rev. William Craven, pastor; Revs. W. D. Cornwell, J. C. Collier and N. Crane, local preachers; R. C. Fritz, superintendent of Sunday School; V. I. Clark, superintendent North Side School; Trustees: A. J. Yaw, W. D. Swail, Walter M. Powers, John C. Longcor, Richard Jarvis, John List, Thomas Cornwell, A. C. Fassett and I. H. Flack; Stewards: A. W. Swift, George M. Marshall, J. W. Sharp, George Hill, Frank Stow, W. M. Sawyer, John L. Collier, W. Dawson, R. C. Fritz, John Fair, Garrett Sager, Levi

REV. C. A. CUMMINGS.

R. Fitzer, George B. Frye. The Ladies Aid Society, the Woman's Foreign and Home Missionary Societies are active in both home and outside benevolent work. The Men's League, organized about two years, has proved a source of interest as well as a very helpful agency in church work amongst men.

FIRST PRESBYTERIAN CHURCH.

CAUGHT BY A KODAK AT THE NORTHWESTERN R. R. BRIDGE.
PHOTO BY W. H. ROBINSON.

The organization of this church was at the log house of Stephen Burnett, three miles north of Belvidere, March 17, 1839, with 24 members, viz.: Ezra May, Mrs. Dorcas May, Stephen Burnett, Mrs. Abigail Burnett, Frederic S. Sheldon, Mrs. Harriet C. Sheldon, George D. Hicks, Mrs. Abigal Hicks, Austin Gardner, Mrs. Mary Gardner, Aaron H. Billings, David Caswell, Chauncy Bristol, Mrs. Louisa Rollins, Mrs. Mary C. Dubois, Mrs. Maria L. Fisk, Mrs. Juliet Gilman, Mrs. Hannah Blood, Mrs. Rulena McBride, Mrs. Nancy Hale, Mrs. Ruth Cunningham, Mrs. Lovina May, Miss Adaline E. Sheldon, Mrs. Gilbert. Rev. John Morrill officiated on this occasion. Ezra May and Austin Gardner were elected ruling elders. In 1839 the church began worship in a public hall, which was occupied for three years. In 1843 the first church edifice of this society, which was the first building in this county used exclusively for church purposes, was erected. In 1857 this was replaced by what is now the main part of the present edifice, at a cost of $18,000. In 1889 this was remodeled, at an expense of $10,000. Present value of the church property including parsonage, $25,000. The following have been pastors of the church: Revs. Royal Nathaniel Wright, Charles Fanning, Eleazer T.

A PRETTY SCENE ON THE KISHWAUKEE RIVER.
PHOTO BY W. H. ROBINSON.

Ball, Henry B. Holmes, David R. Eddy, Thomas C. Easton, Henry M. Curtis, Matthew F. Howie, John H. Windsor, John Clark Hill and George R. Pierce, the present pastor. The elders now serving are: Eli Foote, Henry W. Avery, Daniel E. Foote, Martin C. Bentley, Henry J. Sherill, Edwin W. Warren, Frederic S. Dubois, David D. Sabin and J. C. Zinser. The board of trustees is as follows: E. A. Cleaveland, Enos T. Gage, Albert Scherrer, J. R. Balliet, Joseph E. Tripp, Williard T. Longeor, John C. Foote, George T.

Keator and Sidney A. Sabin. The present membership of the church is 350. The Sunday-school was organized in 1840, Deacon Austin Gardner being the first superintendent. Fourteen persons have officiated as superintendents, Henry W. Avery having served at different times an aggregate of thirty-two years. Eugene F. Sabin is the present superintendent. Total membership of the school 210. A number of societies in charge of the women render valuable service. A fine new pipe-organ was recently placed in the church.

FIRST BAPTIST CHURCH.

The first church in Belvidere was organized July 24, 1836, at the home of Dr. John S. King, and was christened the Belvidere Baptist Church of Christ. This pioneer band numbered sixteen, whose names were: Rev. John S. King, M.D., Nathaniel Crosby, Moses Blood, Melvin Schenck, Calvin Kingsley, Andrew Moss, Timothy Caswell, Caleb Blood, Ira Haskins, Chas. S. Whitman, Mrs. Elizabeth Payne, Mrs. Ann Schenck, Mrs. Charlotte S. Kingsley, Mrs. Mary Caswell, Mrs. Mary Haskins, Miss Matilda Caswell. Its first regular pastor was Prof. S. S. Whitman, whose labors began in October, 1836, in the principal room, sixteen feet square, of a log dwelling house. There followed him Revs. S. A. Estee, C. H. Roe, H. J. Eddy, W. W. Miner, J. P. Phillips, W. A. Welsher, A. C. Keene, Emery Curtis, Jesse Coker, H. C. Mabie, H. W. Reed, J. J. Irving and the present pastor. In 1838 a house of worship, a small frame building, was erected on a lot one block west of the present location. This was also used for many secular purposes. During the pastorate of Rev. Charles Hill Roe, the second church, of brick and costing $5,000, was built on the site of the present edifice. The beautiful and commodious structure now occupied was built in 1867 at an expense of $30,000. It has since been remodeled and decorated. In 1866 letters were granted to sixty-five members, who organized the South Baptist Church. The First Church will mark its 60th anniversary July 24th next. Its record of membership is: Names enrolled, 1600—of these 870 received by baptism and 730 by letters and experience—with a present membership of 295. During the present pastorate now closing its fourth year 101 members have been received. Its Sunday-school numbers 279, and the average attendance is 160. The present officers of the church are: Rev. Romanzo S. Walker, pastor; Frank Sewell, clerk; William H. Robinson, treasurer; William Keeler, William Sewell, G. F. Winnie, L. C. Willard, deacons; John M. Hicks, Sutton Sewell, Jacob Mabie, E. S. Keeler, E. M. Calkins, George Sterling, trustees; B. S. Herbert, J. M. Hicks, finance committee; Frank Sewell, chorister; Alice Rogers, organist; E. S. Keeler, superintendent of Sunday-school. The society is out of debt, harmonious and well organized for church work.

SOUTH BAPTIST CHURCH.

This church was organized October 26, 1865, by sixty-five members, who came from the First Baptist Society. The first church building was erected in 1867 at a cost of $19,000. The first trustees were: A. F. Moss, Samuel Wood, Henry G. Andrews, M. M. Boyce and John Plane. In December, 1871, the first edifice was burned. The second and present structure was dedicated October 9, 1873. The building and furniture cost $16,000. Nine pastors have served the church, their names following: Revs. H. M. Carr, 1865-7; J. L. Benedict (deceased), 1867-8; John Fulton, 1869-76; J. M. Whitehead, 1876-9; W. P. Elsdon, 1880-2; A. C. Peck, 1883-4; C. E. Taylor, 1884-7; E. C. Stover, 1887-90; and the present pastor, whose service began October 19, 1890. During these thirty years there have been baptized 520, received by letter, 223; by experience, 69; a total of 812. There have been excluded 56; dismissed by letter, 265; died 97;

total, 418. Other changes leaves the present membership at 353. The amount of money raised during the same period for all purposes is $95,000. The present church officers are: Rev. James A. Pierce, pastor; H. G. Andrews, E. N. Lincoln, Abram Kipp, Richard T. Hicks, William C. Tullock, deacons; F. W. Plane, A. Hayes, O. J. Lincoln, D. C. Woolverton, C. M. Church, trustees; J. M. Humphrey, clerk; Mrs. F. W. Plane, treasurer; E. J. Watkins, chorister; Mrs. E. J. Watkins, organist; Miss Myrtle McMullen, pianist. The bible school has 15 classes with 25 officers and teachers, and a total enrollment of 250. Mrs. R. E. Osgood has had charge of the primary department for nearly thirty years. The various societies connected with the church work have large memberships, and are in a flourishing condition. The present pastor came from a nearly eight years service at Randolph, Vt., this being his fourth pastorate. He graduated from Colgate University, at Hamilton, N. Y., in 1873, and was ordained in July of the same year. During the current pastorate forty-five have been baptized and thirty received by letter. The congregations have increased, and the general condition of church has been improved.

FREE METHODIST CHURCH.

This church was organized in November, 1860, Rev. E. P. Hart (now senior bishop of the same denomination), being its first pastor. The original membership numbered eleven, which in a brief period increased to forty, and afterward to eighty. For a time the church flourished, but for various reasons, among them removals and changes to other denominations, it became nearly extinct, but it afterward revived and is now in a fairly prosperous condition. The church edifice was purchased of the Congregational society, and the property, at the corner of Main and Perry streets, is valued at $2,250. The present membership is thirty-one, and of the Sabbath-school thirty. The officers are: J. E. Cronk, J. R. Simpson, F. D. Smith, trustees; J. R. Simpson, local preacher; Bertha L. Rubeck, evangelist; Permilia D. Fay, class leader; M. E. Stiles, superintendent of Sabbath-school; T. R. Jackson, W. Cronk, F. Rubeck, Lottie B. Cronk, Carrie Stiles, stewards. A correct list of the pastors cannot be obtained, as the church records have been lost. The present pastor, Rev. J. G. Rockenbach, entered upon his charge October 13, 1895. The pastor and members find great encouragement in the present situation, and look to the future with confidence.

ST. JAMES, CATHOLIC.

St. James Catholic church has a large membership. The Rev. Dr. O'Callaghan is pastor, assisted by Father Murphy. The church edifice is one of the finest in the city. It was impossible to secure any information about the early organization of the church, and also to secure photographs of the pastors.

TRINITY EPISCOPAL CHURCH.

Priest in charge, Rev. C. A. Cummings. The early records of Trinity church were destroyed by fire some years ago. The church was organized previous to 1857. The present building was completed in that year. In its early days Trinity church was very prosperous and so continued until about 1872, when it began to decline, through removals and deaths, and finally services were discontinued. It remained in this condition with an occasional service, until 1893, when a move was made to resume its work. The move proved successful, and it is now a prosperous mission. The building has been thoroughly renovated, additional furniture supplied, regular services kept up, and now it has a settled pastor and a bright outlook for the future. The mission has no indebtedness of any kind. It has 147 members and 82 communicants.

THE GERMAN LUTHERAN CHURCH.

The German Evangelical Lutheran Immanuel church was organized in 1869. Prior to 1893, for about fifteen years, services were held in the old church building on the South Side. In 1893 this property was sold and the present building erected on West Boone street. The value of the church property is about $10,000. The church has a membership of 600. Since 1870, 593 children have been baptized.

There is no Sunday-school, but connected with the church is a parochial day-school, attended by thirty-eight pupils at the present time. Following are the branches taught: Reading, writing, spelling, grammar, translation, United States history, geography, arithmetic — all in English; language, Bible history and catechism, in German; singing of religious hymns, and secular German and English songs. German is spoken for two hours in the morning, English the rest of the day. The present officers are: L. Schult, presiding officer; Charles Braun, Herman Uteg, John Stegeman, elders; August Lettow, Frederick Suhr, August Schwebke, trustees; W. Schult, secretary; John Geick, financial secretary; Herman Ludtke, treasurer. The organist is Miss Caroline Matthies; assistant organist, Master Clemens Heinemann. The church is the proud owner of a pipe organ of local renown. The singing is congregational.

The following pastors have served the church in the order named: Rev. Ph. Estel, now in Southern Illinois; Rev. Steinrauf, now a physician; Rev. C. Eisfeldt, now in South Chicago; Rev. P. Baumgartner, now in Nebraska; Rev. Th. Kohn, now in Chicago; Rev. E. Heinemann, since 1892. The latter was born in Crete, Will county, Illinois; received his education in the parochial schools of Madison county, Illinois, and Ft. Wayne, Indiana; graduated from Concordia College, Ft. Wayne, in 1879, and from Concordia Theological Seminary, St. Louis, in 1882. Among his duties are: Preaching, teaching the parochial school, and instructing and conducting the choir.

GERMAN EVANGELICAL.

The German Evangelical Society was organized September 18, 1867, at a private residence on the corner of Madison and Webster streets, with a membership of eight, viz.: Mr. and Mrs. Fred. Lampert, Mr. and Mrs. Charles Fritz, Mr and Mrs. Jacob Huber, Mr. and Mrs. Fred. Voshage. Its meetings were held at various places until 1873, in which year the society purchased two lots and a residence, and remodeled the latter into a house of worship. In 1888 the present structure was erected, under the pastorate of Rev. J. Alber, and a few years later the parsonage built. The value of the entire property is $6,000. The present church membership is 90, and Sunday-school 100. The church officers are: Fred. Puls, trustee; Fred. Lampert, president; John Sexauer, vice-president; J. G. Meyer, secretary; John H. Luhman, treasurer. Other officers: Fred. Hager, Jr., superintendent Sunday-school; Lena Puls, organist; Fred. Puls, exhorter. Pastors: Revs. V. Forkel, who organized the society; E. Musselman, 1868-9; B. Ruh, 1869-71; Adam Rohrback, 1871-3; L. Willman, 1873-6; L. A. Keller, 1876-9; William Schweiker, 1879-82; Ph. Zahn, 1882-4; Henry Schumacher and L. A. Keller, 1884-6; W. L. Walker, 1886-8; J. Alber, 1888-91; L. Willman, 1891-5. Rev. F. C. Stierle, the present pastor, was appointed to this charge in April, 1895. The society is in a prosperous condition, and has a promising future.

HISTORY OF OUR SCHOOLS.

The early schools were conducted in private residences, and among the first teachers were Miss Harriet King and Miss Rebecca Loop. In 1838 a building was erected by a joint stock company, and called the Newton Academy, on the block now occupied by H. C. DeMunn. S. S. Whitman was the first principal, and had a number of successors until 1852, when Rev. Chas. Hill Roe bought the property and used the Academy building as a residence. In 1842 the public school system was adopted. In 1845 D. B. Pettit opened a school, with eighty-six pupils, in the first Baptist church, elsewhere mentioned. He, with others, taught for some years in the church, the old Academy and residences. A public schoolhouse of stone was built in 1854. In 1857 a brick addition to the latter was completed at a cost of $8,000. In 1895 the original stone structure was torn down and replaced by one of brick, and the entire building remodeled, at an expense of $20,000. The building is now a beautiful structure, and modern in every respect. The most approved hygienic conditions have been observed in the lighting, heating and ventilating. Its ten school-rooms and extra class-rooms are models of convenience and comfort. A fine library and well-supplied laboratory have been provided. The graduates of the high-school are admitted to the Illinois State University without examination. The principal, Professor Horatio A. Warren, is a graduate of Johns Hopkins University, and of fine scholarly attainments. His assistant is Miss Anna McConnell, and the grade teachers are: Misses Flora Fellows, Mary Devlin, Mary Hales, Hattie Webster, Dove Greenlee, Gertrude Saxton, Nellie Gilman and Mrs. Belle Tripp. The number of pupils enrolled is 400, and the average attendance 350. The Board of Education is composed of A. C. Fassett, president; G. H. Hurlbut, secretary; J. W. Sharp, Wm. Sewell, L. C. Willard, Mrs. Gilbert Whitman, Mrs. Alice J. Sherrill.

In South Belvidere the original school building was erected in the early 50's, and remodeled in 1878. A separate new structure was completed in 1894. The total construction outlay has been about $40,000. The number of rooms is thirteen, including a well-equipped laboratory. Every desirable convenience has been provided throughout the buildings. The total enrollment of pupils is 702, and the average attendance 650. The superintendent of schools is Professor R. V. DeGroff, a graduate of the Northwestern University. His executive ability and scholarship are of a high order. The principal of the high school is Miss Carrie Longley, with Miss Mamie Herrick as first assistant. The teachers in the eight grades are: Misses Alice Warren, Ella Hollingshead, Mrs. R. V. DeGroff, Alice Munn, Louisa Morris, Sadie Herrick, Olive Dawson, Mary Hakes, Nellie Adams, Matie Richardson, Grace Hollingshead and Mrs. Esther Thrush.

The cause of education has received constant and loyal support from the people of Belvidere. In rank and thoroughness of method the schools of the city stand in the front line, and are a source of pride and satisfaction to every citizen.

BELVIDERE'S RAILROAD FACILITIES.

The Chicago and Northwestern Railroad Company finished its line to Belvidere in 1852. In 1853 the Madison division was completed. In 1885 was added the Spring Valley division, thus making this point in reality a junction of three lines. In 1893 twenty-seven acres of land were purchased, just north of the river, and a transfer system established. On this tract was erected a main warehouse four hundred feet long, and ten miles of track were laid. Here the enormous business falling to the care of the freight department is transacted, over ten thousand cars per year being handled. The round-house is situated just east of these yards. Twenty-five engines per day, on an average, are here cared for. Nineteen regular passenger trains on each secular day pass this station, together with six on Sunday. The amount of coal used at this station for 1895 was 17,248 tons. The trackage within the city limits is three miles of main and fifteen miles of side, a total of eighteen miles. Mr. Luke Wheeler, station agent and trainmaster at this point, assumed charge in August, 1892. Mr. Wheeler's connection with railroad affairs has extended over a period of thirty-two years. For many years a conductor he was finally stationed at Turner as agent, where he remained ten years, and was then appointed assistant superintendent of the Galena division, with headquarters at Chicago for three years. Preferring a post where the duties would be less exacting, he solicited a change to Belvidere. The responsibilities of the position are great, and require an official of experience, fine executive ability, popular with the public, and one to be relied upon in every emergency. These qualifications are possessed by Mr. Wheeler in an eminent degree. The following are on the staff of the principal officer: Fred Peek, assistant agent, in full charge of freight department; E. Newell, day operator and ticket clerk; L. Newell, night operator; E. R. Bishop, day yardmaster; Samuel Gall, night yardmaster; Lewis Payne, foreman of transfer house; William Hewitt, foreman of round-house; Louis McElroy, roadmaster, Chas. Bruce, baggageman. On the roll of office and yard employes are fifty names. Two hundred pay checks are issued here monthly, twenty-five freight crews being included in the distributing. The service rendered by the company to its patrons here, notwithstanding an absence of competition, has been along the line of intelligent appreciation of the city's needs, and is generally recognized at its full value.

FRATERNAL SOCIETIES.

Evidence of the harmony and social spirit prevailing may be found in the large number of fraternal organizations successfully maintained. The work accomplished, both of a charitable and fraternal nature, is of importance, and its results widespread and effective. The Masons and Oddfellows are the oldest among the societies, both having been formed in 1847. The officers and numerical strength of the different orders are here given:

Belvidere Lodge No. 60, A. F. and A. M. Charter members: A. E. Ames, O. Crosby, N. Hotchkiss, L. Fuller, A. Witter, A. Williams, H. Ripley, J. G. Prentiss. Present officers: F. E. Gilbert, W. M.; F. B. Sands, S. W.; D. Hughes, Jr., J. W.; Fred Sands, Treas.; E. J. Munn, Secy.; F. W. Crain, S. D.; H. W. Davis, J. D.; L. E. Benson, Tyler. Kishwaukee Chapter No. 90, R. A. M.; C. B. Loop, M. E. H. P.; E. E. Spooner, E. King; H. F. Bowley, E. Scribe; E. J. Munn, C. H.; H. H. Rubin, Treas.; C. E. Kelsey, Sec.; J. H. Thomas, P. S.; F. E. Gilbert, R. A. C.; Fred Sands, G. M. 3d Veil; C. L. Smith, G. M. 2nd Veil; B. B. McFall, G. M. 1st Veil; James E. Wheat and J. H. Livingston, Stewards; L. E. Benson, Sentinel; C. E. Kelsey, Organist. Membership 150, total number in city 200.

Big Thunder Lodge No. 28, I. O. O. F. Charter members: D. Howell, A. J. Crosby, N. W. Birge, E. G. Wolcott, J. S. Whitney. Present officers: J. W. Goodwin, N. G.; A. J. Shattuck, V. G.; R. A. Simpson, R. Sec.; H. Weston, P. S.; Walter Lucas, Treas. Membership 98.

G. A. R., Hurlbut Post No. 164. C. B. Loop, Commander; H. H. Hakes, S. V. C.; Garret Depuy, J. V. C.; N. B. Wing, Officer of Day; C. B. Drake, Adjutant; Robt. Horan, Q. M.; Samuel Smith, Officer of Guard. Membership 100.

Sons of Veterans, T. G. Lawler Camp, No. 60. E. W. Doane, Captain; C. Hill, 1st Lieut.; H. I. Haskins, 2d Lieut.; C. T. Spackman, Chaplain; E. B. Harding, 1st Sergt.; F. L. Gilman, Sergt. of Guard; H. Hill, Q. M. Sergt.; O. Schmidt, Color Sergt.; G. H. Hurlbut, Corp. of Guard; A. Steele, Prin. Musician; T. Grow, Camp Guard; C. T. Spackman, C. D. Loop, F. L. Gilman, Camp Council. Membership 36.

A. O. U. W., Belvidere Lodge, No. 152. H. J. Powers, P. M. W.; D. W. Palmer, M. W.; L. H. Whitney, Foreman; Jacob Miller, Overseer; Wm. M. Dawson, Recorder; C. W. Peck, Financier; Frank Sewell, Receiver; F. L. Tanner,

Guide; Samuel Wylde, I. W.; W. H. Cornell, O. W.; G. C. Tallerday, Med. Ex.; W. H. Cornell, Lodge Deputy. Membership 60.

Modern Woodmen, Boone Camp, No. 52. A. C. Fassett, Ven. Consul; A. T. Ames, W. A.; J. L. Collier, W. B.; Otto Schmidt, C.; E. T. Ames, E.; S. E. Leaman, W.; Frank Bahr, S.; A. W. Swift, Physician; Frank King, S. B. Taylor, Wm. P. Merrill, Managers. Membership 240.

Royal Arcanum. L. E. Coleman, Regent; J. D. Peart, V. R.; A. H. Keeler, Orator; O. G. Forrer, P. R.; A. J. Yaw, Sec.; W. L. Wyman, Collector; B. F. Harnish, Treas.; E. L. Barton, Chaplain; F. F. Ross, Guide; C. H. Vail, Warden; A. F. Wheeler, Sentinel. Membership 80.

Knights of Pythias. Wm. Bowley, Chan. Com.; Chas. Cramer, V. C.; Wm. R. Dodge, Prelate; Chas. T. Spackman, M. W.; Max Kunze, K. R. & S.; Fred Marean, M. F.; John Thren, M. E.; Chas. Schaeffer, M. A. Membership 110.

Knights of the Globe. LaFayette Garrison, No. 27. J. L. Collier, S. J.; E. E. Spooner, J.; George Rowley, P.; N. B. Wing, I. P.; F. L. Tanner, A.; James Livingston, C.; William Hancock, E.; D. C. Bishop, L. C. Membership, 75.

Liberty Home Forum, No. 7. Otto Schmidt, Pres.; Mary Orth, 1st V.-P.; Mrs. C. A. Tucker, 2d V.-P.; T. F. Burns, Treas.; C. A. Tucker, Sec.; Emma Wylde, Historian; Amos Bounds, Orator; Anna Youngreen, A. O.; E. M. Styles, Porter; William Johnson, Guard; S. Barney, S. J. Hicks, S. Wylde, Directors. Membership, 75.

Knights of the Maccabees. Kishwaukee Tent, No. 61. T. L. Manley, P. S. K. C.; A. Scherrer, S. K. C.; B. R. Lear, S. K. L. C.; R. S. Hopkins, R. & F. K.; Charles Lanning, Chaplain; Dr. Carpenter, Physician; Charles Derthick, Sergt.; W. A. Gleason, M. A.; A. D. Green, 1st M. G.; J. Reno, 2d M. G.; Axel Ahlsen, S.; S. L. Devlin, P. Membership, 40.

American Legion of Honor. D. D. Sabin, Com.; L. H. Murch, V.-C.; E. L. Murch, O.; G. W. Murch, P. C.; J. R. Balliet, Sec.; Enos T. Gage, Coll.; R. J. Tousley, Treas.; R. E. Osgood, Chaplain; T. F. Butler, G.; I. H. Flack, W.; Robt. Banwell, S. Membership, 26.

National Union. Belvidere Council, No. 543. J. F. Hannah, Pres.; A. R. Guillow, V.-Pres.; H. E. Babcock, S.; N. S. Thompson, Ex-Pres.; Charles Beverly, Sec.; F. W. Crain, F. S.; Josiah Dempsey, Treas.; I. A. Holcomb, Chaplain; G. M. Elliott, Usher; Charles Ehrlinger, S. of A.; E. E. Yontz, D.; D. M. Eldredge, G. M. Elliott, A. R. Hopkins, Trustees; C. L. Eldredge, Dist. Dpty. Membership, 47.

I. O. Foresters. Court Clair, No. 183. Louis Dovenmuhle, C. R.; W. Eisenstein, V. C. R.; E. Lembachner, F. S.; James Tynau, R. S.; J. H. Downs, Treas.; H. Keorting, J. W.; E. Smith, S. W.; F. McGouigle, J. B.; C. Thurlby, S. B.; A. Phillips, R. S. P. Membership, 43.

Besides the above there are benevolent associations among the railroad and factory men, and in connection with the various churches.

A number of literary and musical organizations have fair memberships.

LADIES' LYRIC CLUB.

The Ladies' Lyric Club was organized January, 1894, and numbers about fifty active and six associate members. The aim in organizing such a society was not only a development of a higher musical taste in the community, but for the advancement in musical culture of its members. The officers of the club are: Mrs. Jennie C. Ramsey, president; Mrs. Lillie G. Gage, vice-president; Mrs. Ella Plane, secretary; Mrs. Jennie H. Hannah, treasurer; Miss Bertha Loop, accompanist.

THE MAMMOTH FACTORY AND PLANT OF THE NATIONAL SEWING MACHINE CO.

THE NATIONAL SEWING MACHINE COMPANY.

HISTORY OF THIS GREAT INDUSTRY FROM ITS INCEPTION TO THE PRESENT TIME.
THE PRIDE OF BELVIDERE AND THE PALLADIUM OF HER INDUSTRIAL FUTURE.

A veritable colossus of industrial extant and import, of evidence and influence in the commercial world, the great National Sewing Machine Manufactory of Belvidere stands to-day a living monument to tireless energy, perfect organization, shrewd management, unerring judgment and the keenest business sagacity; and all

B. ELDREDGE.
PRESIDENT OF THE NATIONAL SEWING MACHINE CO.
PHOTO BY YOUNDT.

this due, more than from any other circumstance or cause, to the earnest, conscientious effort and determination of one man, dominated by that unquenchable "I will" spirit that knows no barriers, that comprehends no such word as fail; that same persevering faith that has made Chicago to-day the wonder and admiration of two hemispheres, and within the past few decades caused the hills and plains of this boundless western country to "blossom like the rose."

The substance of past success and the manifestness of present achievement speak louder than can any words for the reputation of the National factory, and in this industry we recognize the security of our city's future prosperity and im-

THE ELDREDGE.
THE HANDSOMEST HIGH GRADE WHEEL MADE.

portance as a manufacturing center. That its record of past accomplishments presages still greater works and consequent increased emoluments, none can doubt who are even in a small measure conversant with the history of the concern. Small wonder then that the 8,000 citizens of Belvidere point with pride—a pardonable pride—to this immense industrial institution, which furnishes employment and a means of support for over fifty per cent. of the population. A manufactory such as this would be an honor to any city in the land. It is at the present time, with the added improvements of which we shall speak later on, the largest and most completely equipped bicycle plant in the United States, as well as the second largest sewing machine factory in the world.

LADY ELDREDGE.
THE NATIONAL COMPANY'S LEADING LADIES' BICYCLE.

THE BELVIDERE.
AN HONEST HIGH GRADE BICYCLE THAT HAS FEW EQUALS.

SUBSTANTIATED THEIR CLAIMS.

The success of this enterprise has been particularly gratifying to the citizens of Belvidere, because they have long believed that this city possessed advantages which should make it one of the leading manufacturing centers of the state and the west, and can now present convincing and conclusive evidence in support of

THE ELDREDGE B. SEWING MACHINE.

34 BELVIDERE ILLUSTRATED.

their claims. They also find a large measure of satisfaction in the fact that an enterprise which in Chicago was conducted with indifferent success has been phenomenally successful in Belvidere. This fact alone ought to encourage other manufactories to locate here.

The history of the building up of this establishment is one of more than ordinary interest, because it is the history of the building up of a new industry in competition with those controlled by old, wealthy and powerful corporations. It

DAVID PATTON,
SECRETARY OF THE NATIONAL SEWING MACHINE CO.
PHOTO BY YOUNDT.

is the history of determined, persistent and unceasing effort on the part of its chief promoters, when they were beset by difficulties which at times seemed to be insurmountable and practically beyond solution.

THE JUNE MANUFACTURING COMPANY.

Summarizing this history it may be said that something like a dozen years since Frank T. June was at the head of a company, engaged in a small way in manufacturing in Chicago, at the corner of La Salle and Ontario streets, the old Singer sewing machine, patents on which had expired, and the Jennie June, a machine developed by the president of the company. The June Manufacturing

Company was the name by which the concern was known at the time. It labored under the difficulty of not being able to turn out a machine satisfactory to the public when compared with later inventions in the same line. About the same time Barnabas Eldredge, also of Chicago, a man of large experience in the handling and sale of improved sewing machines, was endeavoring to introduce into the market a machine which, while it was not entirely his own invention, had been developed under his direction and bore his name. This was a superior kind of machine in which the old manufacturers having a monopoly of the trade recognized a dangerous competitor. Not having the means to manufacture this machine on his own account, Mr. Eldredge was contracting the manufacture to eastern parties.

VIEW IN PRIVATE OFFICE OF B. ELDREDGE,
PRESIDENT OF THE NATIONAL SEWING MACHINE CO.
PHOTO BY CLARK & NOTT.

Being continually disappointed and hampered in his operations by reason of not being able to personally supervise the construction of his machine, Mr. Eldredge went to Mr. June and entered into an agreement to have his machines made by the latter, on contract, in Chicago. This agreement continued in effect for some time, and then Mr. Eldredge proposed a consolidation of interests, which was accomplished and went into effect in the early part of 1885. They were hardly started under the new regime when the labor troubles of that year, culminating in the anarchist riots, involved them in a controversy with their employes and closed their factory.

THE PLANT REMOVED TO BELVIDERE.

This forced upon them the consideration of a new problem, and for a time they were at sea as to what course they should pursue. It was at this juncture that a suggestion came to them that they should remove their plant to Belvidere, where it was urged they would be free from the influences leading up to strikes, a perpetual menace to the industrial interests of Chicago. In pursuance of this suggestion negotiations were begun in July, 1886, with some of Belvidere's enterprising citizens, who offered the company substantial aid and encouragement, and in a short time arrangements for the removal were completed. The June Manufacturing Co., with a capital of $250,000, was incorporated under the laws of Illinois, with $130,000 paid-in stock. Mr. June was elected president, and Mr. Eldredge, vice-president and general manager. The erection of a factory was begun at once, and in the latter part of the following November the first manufacturing enterprise of any magnitude ever launched in Belvidere went into operation with 175 em-

A PORTION OF MAIN OFFICE.
NATIONAL SEWING MACHINE CO.
PHOTO BY CLARK & NOTT.

ployes on its pay-roll. Thus, indirectly, the labor strikes of Chicago sent to Belvidere what is now by far its greatest manufactory.

CONFRONTED BY A PROBLEM.

With these operations the solution of an important problem began. The problem to be solved was, whether a new sewing machine factory, located in a territory where the experiment had not been before tried, and with limited resources, could survive the assaults of the old manufacturing companies, having a practical monopoly of the trade, with unlimited capital at their command, and united in their determination to keep new competitors out of the field. The public is so familiar with the methods of this old sewing machine combination that it is hardly necessary to say that the chances were largely against the new aspirant for popular favor and public patronage. For a time the results seemed to be quite uncertain and the citizens of Belvidere, deeply interested as they were in the success of the enterprise, were at times somewhat doubtful on this point, but the subsequent history of this great concern has proven how utterly groundless were their doubts and fears.

RECOGNIZED ON ITS MERITS.

The one man among those interested in this undertaking, who appears never to have yielded, even temporarily, to discouragement was Mr. Eldredge. Although not the official head of the corporation, he was the man most familiar with the sewing machine business, best acquainted with the demands of the public and most fully informed as to the avenues available for conveying their manufactures into

OFFICES OF W. S. BROWN,
SUPERINTENDENT OF NATIONAL SEWING MACHINE CO

the market. Under his direction a machine was manufactured which compelled recognition of its merits, and advertised its manufacturers. It went into the market to make new friends and to bring new patrons to the factory, with a corresponding increase of business. At first the increase was slow, but it was a steady and continuous increase, and nothing once gained was sacrificed through inattention to anything which their patrons seemed to demand.

AN IMPORTANT CHANGE.

In 1890 Mr. June died and Mr. Eldredge succeeded to the presidency, redoubling at once his efforts to expand the business and enlarge the trade, which at this time had begun to assume important proportions. His son, Franklin P. Eldredge, became vice-president, and David Patton became secretary. The name was changed to the National Sewing Machine Company, and if there is aught in a name that was most certainly a fortunate choice, for the past five years have been the most prosperous and brilliant in the history of the company. Up to the present time the output of the factory since locating here, amounts, in round numbers, to over 600,000 sewing machines of various kinds, and the best evidence of the general prosperity of the enterprise is found in the fact that the stock of the company now commands a premium of more than one hundred per cent.

A WINNING POLICY.

From the moment almost that Mr. Eldredge assumed the management of the factory and was left unhampered to follow his ideas as to how the affairs of such a concern should be conducted to attain the best results, the business received im-

OFFICE OF E. E. MANNING,
MANAGER OF SHIPPING DEPARTMENT OF NATIONAL SEWING MACHINE CO.
PHOTO BY CLARK & NOTT.

mediately a decided impetus, and so rapidly increased as to surprise even the officers of the company, who, while sanguine of ultimate success, hardly looked so soon for such a positive and favorable response to the new policy of the management. This new policy was broad and comprehensive in the fullest sense of the term—a reaching out for new business far and near, and introducing of goods into territory which formerly the Company had been unable to reach through force of circumstances. Energy and "push," begotten of fullest confidence in the quality and excellence of goods manufactured, strict attention to detail, and an absolute fairness in dealing with customers, small and great, soon turned the tide in favor of the Company, and Mr. Eldredge soon saw the fruits of his years of labor and planning manifest in the factory running to its fullest capacity. The only trouble was in filling the multitudinous orders that poured in. By degrees the plant was enlarged to accommodate the rapidly growing trade, and from 175 employes in

1886 the force had increased to nearly 700 in 1894, while the capacity of the works had grown to the extent of 75,000 machines annually.

THE NATIONAL'S PROUD FAME.

Such excellent and universal satisfaction did the National sewing machines give that wherever they were sold came repeated demands for more. The very name of the Company on any machine was sufficient guarantee of its superiority, and the general public was not slow to recognize that fact. This is none the less true to-day. It is, however, but the just reward of genius, perseverance and enterprise; and now, at home and abroad, no sewing machine company in the world

DIRECTORS' ROOM.
NATIONAL SEWING MACHINE CO.
PHOTO BY CLARK & NOTT.

has a more enviable reputation or a prouder fame than the National, both for the quality of its product and its manner of doing business, nor does the name of any man engaged in the manufacture of sewing machines stand out more prominently or command greater respect than that of Barnabas Eldredge.

DIFFERENT MACHINES MADE.

At the present time the company is manufacturing the Eldredge, the Belvidere, the Maywood, the Grand, the Seamstress, and an automatic chain-stitch machine, all different in construction, while they also manufacture machines for other institutions. As Mr. Eldredge often expresses it, "We make these machines from the pig-iron up," and a visit to their enormous plant will convince the most skeptical of the truth of this assertion. As to the style, grade and finish of their machines and the superb cabinet work, hundreds of thousands of housekeepers in this and other lands will testify to the truth of the Company's claim that their line is unequalled.

MAKE THEIR OWN ATTACHMENTS.

Another feature about the National that no other factory can boast of is that it is the only concern of its kind in the world making its own attachments. These attachments are the inventions of Frank L. Goodrich, who at the present time is connected with the Company in the capacity of purchasing agent. They are cov-

A GLIMPSE, OF THE TOOL ROOM, WESTERN AISLE.
NATIONAL SEWING MACHINE CO.
PHOTO BY CLARK & NOTT.

ered by twelve patents, and are universally acknowledged to be the most ingenious, most complete and most satisfactory set of attachments used in connection with any sewing machine made—the delight of the seamstress and the pride of the manufacturers. Mr. Goodrich had an exhibit of his attachments at the World's Fair, and was awarded the first and only prize given—a handsome gold medal—for the best and most complete up-to-date sewing machine attachments shown. He also received from the Board of Lady Managers a diploma of honorary mention, given to those only who were instrumental in perfecting the exhibits of others. These honors were very gratifying to Mr. Goodrich, as well as to the Company, as the recognition of the superiority of the attachments used on their machines gave them a prestige and standing possessed by no other sewing machine concern.

WORLD'S FAIR HONORS.

Mr. Goodrich's attachments were but auxiliary, however, to the magnificent exhibit of sewing machines made by the Company at the great exposition. Their display was one of the finest made by any sewing machine company, and they received more first awards—medals and diplomas—for strictly family sewing machines than any other exhibitor in the same class. Altogether the National Sewing Machine Company received eleven awards, including those of Mr. Goodrich's, and had the proud distinction of being thus honored more than any other

SECTION OF PUNCH PRESS ROOM.
NATIONAL SEWING MACHINE CO.
PHOTO BY CLARK & NOTT.

sewing machine company in the world. Thus it will be seen that the Company's experience at the World's Fair was but the logical sequence of the truth that genuine merit in sewing machines, as well as in human character, wins every time. It was the climax to the verdict of superiority which the public had for years bestowed upon their machines.

THE BICYCLE PLANT.

DESCRIPTION OF THIS GREAT BRANCH OF THE INDUSTRY IN ALL ITS BEARINGS.

And not alone does the National Company manufacture sewing machines. It has in the short space of a year and a half grown to be one of the greatest, if not the greatest, bicycle manufactory in the country. So marvelously successful were the National sewing machines in the markets of the world, in competition with other makes, that the company conceived the idea in the early spring of 1894 of engaging in the manufacture of bicycles, and forthwith "shied their castor into the ring." They commenced work in this department in a small way May 1st of the same year. Their one idea in this connection was that if they manufactured bicycles to any extent the wheel that they should make would be as near the acme of perfection, from a mechanical standpoint, as it were possible to make; a wheel "made upon honor" in every sense of the word; a wheel that with a single bound should take rank with any bicycle made, no matter by whom. To start with, the incomparable reputation achieved by the Company in the manufacture of sewing machines gave them an advantageous position in the business world enjoyed by comparatively few of the wheel-making firms, and it was therefore but natural

EAST END OF MILLING AND DRILLING DEPARTMENT.
NATIONAL SEWING MACHINE CO.
PHOTO BY CLARK & NOTT.

that any bicycle bearing their name should be looked upon with favor by both the big dealers and the public. The first bicycles manufactured by them were so cordially received that they concluded to at once commence their manufacture on a large scale, and in August, 1894, purchased the plant of the Freeport Bicycle Manufacturing Company, and removed it to Belvidere, occupying the three-story brick building just east of their foundry. They commenced at once to turn out bicycles in earnest. These wheels sold like hot cakes, and the success of this new enterprise was assured from the very first. So rapidly did the business grow that it became necessary within a comparatively short time to increase the number of hands in this department from 25 to 100, new machinery was added, and yet the company could not keep up with the orders, which fairly rained in. The Belvidere wheel seemed to be just what the public had been long waiting for; it met the popular taste. The superior quality of material used in the construction of these wheels, the graceful, bird-like lines upon which they were built, the elegance of finish, their easy-running qualities, strength and durability, all combined to make them in immediate and great demand, and it was but a brief space of time before other bicycle manufacturers, and cyclists in general all over the country, became aware of the fact that "we make wheels, too."

POINTS OF STRENGTH.

The three cardinal points of strength that the public immediately recognized in the Belvidere wheels were their beauty, strong construction and smooth running nature—a most happy combination of the practical and essential features to be taken into consideration in wheel-building and in the selection of a wheel.

WEST END MILLING AND DRILLING DEPARTMENT.
NATIONAL SEWING MACHINE CO.
PHOTO BY CLARK & NOTT.

FIRST YEAR'S BUSINESS.

During the year just past – the season of '95 – the Company manufactured and sold 10,000 wheels, a phenomenal record and one never equaled by any bicycle manufacturing concern in its first year's history. They could as easily have sold ten times as many if they had had the facilities for making them. This has been the subject of much favorable comment in the cycling world and in journals devoted to the interest of wheelmen. The leading newspapers of Chicago and the west have also frequently made complimentary mention of this fact. Certainly for an "infant" it is a great record, and one to which even the oldest wheel-building establishment might point with pride. And the most gratifying feature of the whole matter is that the wheels have given entire satisfaction; no first year wheel was ever so enthusiastically received. Dealers who handled the Belvidere wheel last season will be the heaviest buyers in '96, which is the best criterion of its popularity with the masses.

COMPELLED TO ENLARGE.

It became evident to Mr. Eldredge in the early part of the past summer that the quarters then occupied by the bicycle plant would be altogether inadequate to accommodate the rapidly growing business and the still greater increase which was bound to come. Preparations were at once commenced for the erection of a mammoth three-story building fronting on State street, with wings at each end connecting with the old building (as shown in the accompanying illustration), to be used in the main for the manufacture of bicycles. This would give them 100,000 ad-

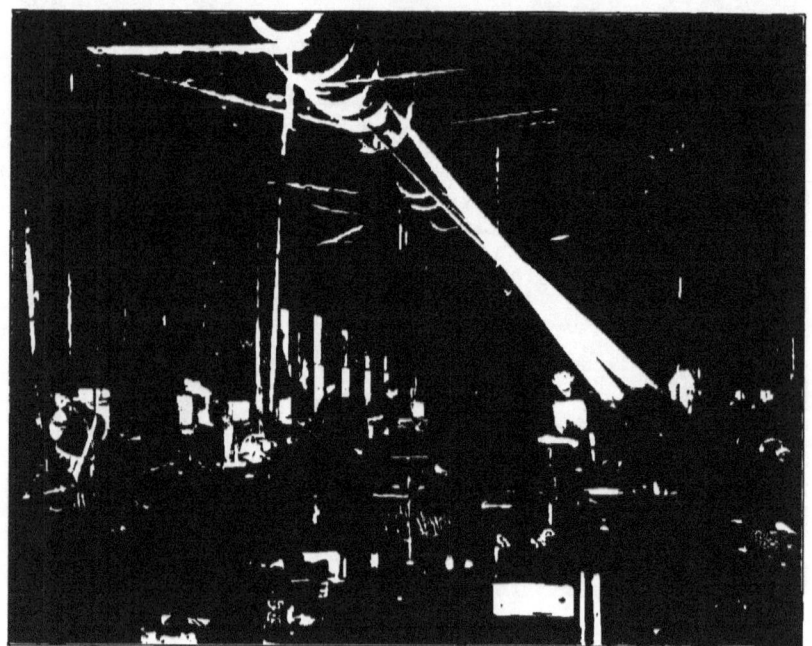

SOUTH QUARTER OF THE LATHE ROOM,
NATIONAL SEWING MACHINE CO.
PHOTO BY CLARK & NOTT.

ditional square feet of floor space and enlarge their producing capacity to 60,000 bicycles per year, if run the year round.

SOME UNWRITTEN HISTORY.

In this connection it might be stated that plans for a building about one-half the size of that above mentioned were drawn up three years ago, the Company at that time intending to build in anticipation of still further enlarging their sewing machine business, and to give them more room for manufacturing purposes, which was even then badly needed. But a condition of things just at that period arose which put a damper on the building prospect and checked the plans of the Company in that direction. The election of Grover Cleveland as president and the return of the democrats to power filled Mr. Eldredge's mind with distrust, as it did that of every great manufacturer in the country; the attitude of the party on the tariff question being responsible for this. Mr. Eldredge foresaw what afterwards happened and is still a condition—the utter incompetency of the democrats in dealing with questions affecting our country's prosperity and in handling the reins of government; their infamous thrusts at the industries of the United States through the Wilson tariff bill; the subsequent terrible financial panic, business depression and closing down of manufacturing plants throughout the land. This Mr. Eldredge knew would affect the National Sewing Machine Company of Belvidere in like proportion with every industry in the country, and consequently wisely concluded not to build "until the clouds rolled by." With the great republican victories of 1894 and the positive assurance they gave of the grand old party's re-

NORTH QUARTER OF LATHE ROOM.
NATIONAL SEWING MACHINE CO.
PHOTO BY CLARK & NOTT.

turn to power in 1896 came returning confidence. The business horizon brightened and the outlook in the commercial world became more hopeful. These facts, coupled with the remarkable success scored by the Company in less than a year in the manufacture of bicycles, crystallized the plan for building, and on April 1st of last year ground was broken and work commenced on the great structure of which we have previously spoken. It took a small army of men seven months to complete it.

THE NEW ADDITION.

This building is immense and imposing, three stories in height and has a frontage on State street of 300 feet. The south wing faces Meadow street, while the north wing looks upon the placid bosom of the Kishwaukee river. At the southwest corner rises a handsome tower from which floats a large flag of the national colors. In the construction of this building over 3,000,000 brick were used. The front is of selected cream-colored brick, manufactured in Belvidere at the brick yards of R. C. Fritz. The remaining walls, chimneys and the huge smoke-stacks are built of brick manufactured at Dundee. In size this new addition to the factory is equal to a one-story building 2,500x40 feet. Something of its magnitude may be gained from this comparison. In it are the private offices of the officials and superintendent, the main office, tool room, polishing room, shipping room, the great bicycle assembling room, 240x80 feet (the largest in the country), store and stock rooms and other departments. Everything about the building, even to the most minute detail, is arranged with an eye to convenience and to best answer the purpose intended.

NORTH-WEST QUARTER OF SEWING MACHINE ASSEMBLING ROOM,
NATIONAL SEWING MACHINE CO.
PHOTO BY CLARK & NOTT.

THE OFFICES.

The private office of the officials of the Company, with the exception of Secretary Patton's, are in the tower, and are models of elegance and convenient arrangement—in keeping with the magnitude and importance of such a vast establishment. They are spacious, well lighted and well apart from the general noise and confusion, giving the officers a privacy in the execution of the multifarious duties that heretofore they have not enjoyed. The floors in these offices are of hard wood with parquetry borders, a fancy design of inlaid wood of different colors; the remainder of the woodwork is of quarter-sawed polished oak; the walls are a light buff in color and stippled; the ceilings are finished in lincrusta-walton design. Each office has an elaborate mantel and a tile fire-place. The walls are adorned with handsome pictures and beautiful rugs cover the floor. Electricity and gas for illuminating, hot water for heating purposes, and speaking tubes connecting with the floor below add still further to the luxuriousness and convenience of the apartments. President B. Eldredge's office occupies the southeast corner, facing on State and Meadow streets and connecting with it on the east are the offices of Vice President E. P. Eldredge and F. L. Goodrich in the order named. On the first floor underneath these offices are Superintendent Brown's headquarters and the draughting room in connection. These are specially arranged for the convenience of the superintendent and his assistants. A hallway separates the private offices upstairs from the main office on the north. This is an immense room to be used for distinctly office purposes and faces to the west on State street. Its dimensions

VIEW IN WEST HALF OF SEWING MACHINE ASSEMBLING DEPARTMENT.
NATIONAL SEWING MACHINE CO.
PHOTO BY CLARK & NOTT.

are 40x80 feet and there is no question but that it is one of the most finely appointed offices in the country. Double standing desks, and other appurtenances that tend to lighten and make pleasant the duties of the clerical force, are used in this department. It is splendidly lighted and is heated and illuminated the same as the private offices. Off from this room to the east is a massive vault, whose great stability is significantly suggestive of the Company's solidity and imperturbability in the commercial world. On the south side of the room is a long stationary desk used by the cashier, at the west end of which is the private office of Secretary Patton. All the furniture, desks, etc., are of quarter-sawed oak finely made and elegantly finished. In connection are toilet rooms for both ladies and gentlemen, modern in every particular and faultlessly appointed. In this main office forty persons are employed in various clerical capacities.

WHO THE BUILDERS WERE.

George H. Bradley & Son, of Rockford, were the architects of this greatest addition to the plant of the National Sewing Machine Company.

John Alexander, of Rockford, had the contract for the mason work, and the building itself is the best evidence of the thoroughness with which he superintended its erection. Every line, every inch from the foundation up, bespeaks the careful eye of an able, experienced contractor and the workmanship of men skilled in their vocation.

The contract for the carpenter work was intrusted to the hands (and head) of Fred H. Dixon, of Belvidere, and it is doubtful if another man could have been

A GLANCE INTO SEWING MACHINE JAPAN AND ORNAMENTING ROOM.
NATIONAL SEWING MACHINE CO.
PHOTO BY CLARK & NOTT.

secured, far or near, who would have given such excellent and complete satisfaction as did Mr. Dixon.

WHEEL OUTPUT FOR '96.

With the erection of this new building and the acquisition of 100,000 additional square feet of floor space, the capacity for bicycle making in this concern is increased at least 500 per cent, which in all probability will be sufficient to meet any demands made upon the Company for several years to come, at least. For the season of '96 the Company has orders booked for 38,000 bicycles, to be made and delivered between November 1, 1895, and July 1, 1896. This is not an estimate of the number of wheels that will be made at the factory this season, but the *actual number* that have already been ordered. Not a half dozen other manufactories in the United States will turn out as many wheels as that in '96.

It is neither probable that the Company will close the season for manufacturing wheels on July 1. On the contrary, it is altogether likely that between that time and the first of the following November they will manufacture an additional 10,000 bicycles, increasing the total output for '96 to 48,000—more wheels than any other bicycle manufacturing concern ever dared to dream of turning out in its second year. The demand for the Belvidere wheel from all parts of the United States speaks louder for its merits and superiority than any effusive words of praise that we might here bestow upon it. The public is not slow to recognize a good thing; the success of the Belvidere wheel was instantaneous with its appearance in the market. The Company last season had to turn away orders for thousands upon thousands of bicycles, and that the first year.

NORTH-EAST PORTION OF POLISHING DEPARTMENT.
NATIONAL SEWING MACHINE CO.
PHOTO BY CLARK & NOTT.

THE MACHINERY USED.

The plant of the National Sewing Machine Company includes the finest line of machinery, tools, gauges, patterns, etc., that money will buy, and their product possesses the best practical features known to modern manufacture. They employ constantly a board of mechanical experts for devising improvements, and maintain a rigid inspection of every part of their sewing machines and bicycles, subjecting them to the severest tests before shipment.

POINTS OF CONSTRUCTION.

As to the construction of the wheels made by the company we quote from their handsomely printed and illustrated catalogue as follows:

"A successful experience of over twenty-five years in manufacturing fine family sewing machines has taught us the best material to use for any particular purpose, and the most successful manner in which to work it. The capability of our factory is very great, and no difficulty will be experienced in building anything in the general manufacturing line, be it sewing machines, fire arms, type writers or high grade bicycles. Is it not reasonable to suppose that a concern which has been successful in one line of manufacturing that requires very close and accurate work will be able to succeed as well in another that requires the same class of labor, the same machinery, and the same close attention to mechanical niceties?

"In building our bicycles we have carefully avoided the general tendency to compromise the vital features of practical construction in order to cater to some

A GLANCE INTO THE GRINDING ROOM.
NATIONAL SEWING MACHINE CO.
PHOTO BY CLARK & NOTT.

fad. We have, however, embodied all the latest improvements, and have followed fashion to the extent of giving latest designs in frames, light weights, narrow tread and large size tubing. Do not be deceived by manufacturers that pretend to have secret processes for treating their materials, and who, therefore, claim to produce a superior article. We have no secrets whatever, no special processes, and our factory is always open in all departments to the inspection of visitors. If we wish to harden a piece of steel we buy the best the market affords, heat it red hot, and cool it in either water or oil, as the case may require.

"The art of bicycle building has been pervaded with altogether too much mystery; there is nothing about wheel building but what is straight, plain work that any first-class mechanic is capable of performing successfully if he is provided with suitable tools and material. We have the mechanics, tools (including finest machinery, complete sets of special gauges, etc.), and material as well as the ability and desire to do the very best class of work possible; hence, our bicycles are strictly high-grade in every particular."

The above frank and straightforward statement of the manner in which their wheels are made is characteristic of the Company's manner of doing business, and it is this one thing as much as any other that has augmented their success and is responsible for the proud position which the industry to-day occupies in Belvidere and the world at large.

STYLES OF WHEELS MADE.

In the plant of the National Sewing Machine Company are manufactured the now famous "Belvidere" and "Eldredge" bicycles in fifty different styles and

PORTION OF THE PLATING DEPARTMENT.
NATIONAL SEWING MACHINE CO.
PHOTO BY CLARK & NOTT.

varying weights. These wheels are now being turned out at the rate of 250 per day; and in point of durability, style and finish—the *tout ensemble*—are the equal of, if not superior to, any wheel on the market to-day. This is not an idle boast; it is a simple fact that is being demonstrated every day in a thousand towns and cities where the Belvidere wheel is ridden. A strong wheel, a beautiful wheel, an honest wheel, a *fin de siecle* wheel in every particular—it leads them all.

For the manufacture of bicycle parts over $100,000 worth of new automatic machinery has just been added to the plant. This is all of the latest and most approved pattern, and turns out the most delicate parts with an accuracy and speed that is simply marvelous. The *modus operandi* of this machinery is wonderful, and these quietly running combinations of wheels and drills and cutting tools, as they produce the finished product, seem possessed of almost human intelligence.

THE PLANT IN GENERAL.

A DETAILED DESCRIPTION OF THE AUXILIARY FEATURES OF THE FACTORY.

The plant of the National Sewing Machine Company is composed of thirteen different buildings, covering eight acres, with six acres of floor space, amounting to nearly 250,000 square feet. These buildings, while used for separate and distinct purposes, are in reality one great building, joined together for convenience sake. Altogether they would make a building 4350x40 feet, one story in height. Something of the immensity of the plant may be had from this comparison.

Aside from the large building just completed the Company erected another

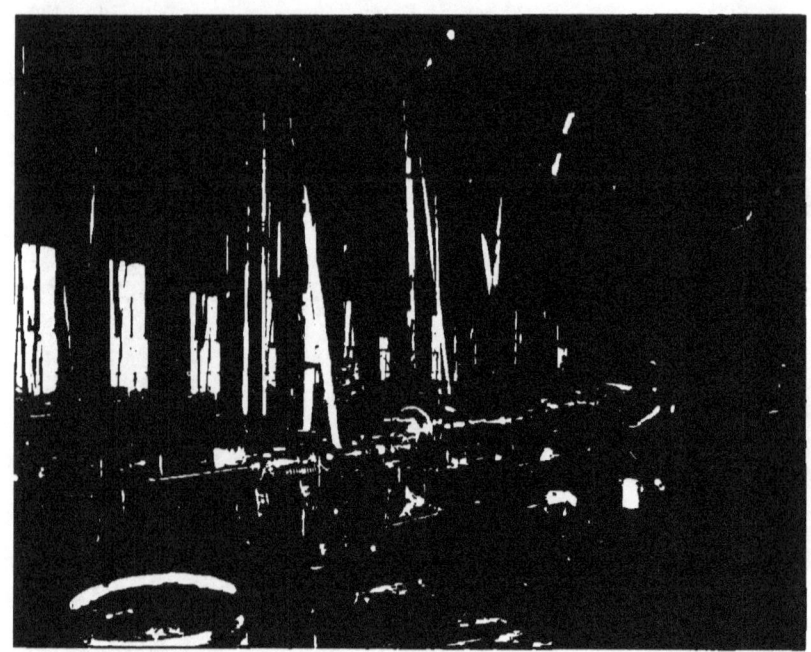

THE AUTOMATIC SCREW MACHINES.
Wonders of modern invention. In this room over seventy in operation.
NATIONAL SEWING MACHINE CO.
PHOTO BY CLARK & NOTT.

structure on the grounds, 150x75 feet and two stories in height, to which the japan and enameling department were transferred as soon as it was finished. In addition to this a new boiler house has just been built and several new boilers also put in.

In round numbers the total cost of building improvements made last year will be fully $100,000.

NUMBER OF EMPLOYES.

The working force now numbers over 1,200. In this connection is a noteworthy fact; the average pay of these men is greater than that received by any other manufacturing concern in the state of Illinois, which assertion can be proven by referring to statistics bearing upon this point, and explains in a measure why the Company each week receives hundreds of applications from men desirous of obtaining work in the factory.

So closely interwoven are the two branches of manufacture in this establishment that no certain figures can be given as to the number of men employed respectively on sewing machine and bicycle work, from the fact that in nearly every department the same men are engaged on both kinds of work.

HARD TIMES NOT FELT.

The best evidence of the prosperous condition of the Company's affairs, and the indisputable wisdom of Mr. Eldredge's business policy at all times and under all circumstances is to be had from the fact that during the business depression and financial panic of '93 and '94, when on every hand were failures, and industries

WEST END OF AUTOMATIC SCREW ROOM.
NATIONAL SEWING MACHINE CO.
PHOTO BY CLARK & NOTT.

shutting down, and hard times, the National Sewing Machine factory continued to "do business at the old stand," with no interruption worth mentioning, and furnished employment for 600 men. While all around us was suffering and hardships such as the people of this country never before knew or were ever called upon to endure, Belvidere was in the midst of peace and plenty and scarcely felt the effects of the hard times. This enviable state of affairs was directly due to the healthful condition of the company's business and the wise judgment of the men at its head in a time when the present gave no certainty and the future bore no confident promise. Had the factory been compelled to shut down during those never to-be forgotten hard times Belvidere would have received a touch of the then prevalent "depression" that it would never have forgotten, but which, let us be thankful a thousand times over to the success of our chief industry, it was spared.

WHO OWNS THE STOCK.

The stock of this vast business is all owned by persons in Belvidere. About 75 per cent is held by B. Eldredge, Mrs. B. Eldredge, F. P. Eldredge and Mrs. F. P. Eldredge. The remaining 25 per cent is held by parties connected with the factory and outside prominent citizens. Just what premium the stock commands it is hard to state, but it is fully or even more than 100 per cent. The quickest and perhaps the surest way of finding out is to approach a stockholder and attempt to purchase a small block. The Company is capitalized at $500,000, with $350,000 paid in, and a working capital of $1,000,000.

SECTION OF THE BIG FOUNDRY.
NATIONAL SEWING MACHINE CO.
PHOTO BY CLARK & NOTT.

FIRE PROTECTION.

The factory is furnished with an elaborate and complete system of fire protection. It is equipped throughout with the Grinnell Automatic Fire Sprinkler system—an arrangement of pipes overhead with a sprinkler every ten feet in each direction, so constructed that should a fire start in any part of the building, as soon as the heat reaches 155 degrees it melts certain parts and sets the sprinklers thus affected by the heat to working automatically, drowning out the blaze in short order. An automatic gong also tells the location of the fire. In addition to this the plant is equipped with another complete system of fire protection in the shape of a network of pipes from the city water-works on the grounds, with hydrants, water plugs, hose and all other fire-fighting paraphernalia that could be called into requisition in a brief space of time if necessary. This fire protection system is under the management of the Superintendent of the Water-works, E. E. Spooner. The factory also has its own fire company drilled and in readiness to fight any flames that may chance to break loose. So well supplied are the grounds with hydrants that it would hardly be possible in any of the buildings to get 150 feet distant from one. Nothing short of a universal spontaneous combustion or an instantaneous conflagration in every part of the plant at once could ever destroy it, so perfectly is it protected from fire.

FINELY ILLUMINATED.

The factory is splendidly lighted by both gas and electricity. The former is furnished by the Belvidere Gas Company, and 30,000 feet per day is used for

AT WORK IN THE SEWING MACHINE SHIPPING DEPARTMENT.
NATIONAL SEWING MACHINE CO.
PHOTO BY CLARK & NOTT.

illuminating and for purposes where great heat is required, such as brazing bicycle frames and heating the enameling ovens. The Company operates its own electric light plant, also a gas plant of its own, and uses both arc and incandescent lights in addition to gas, making it altogether one of the most brilliantly illuminated manufacturing plants at night in the country. The factory, aside from the offices, is heated by a system of steam pipes, and an even temperature is thus afforded, even in the coldest weather, making it a comfortable and most desirable place in which to work.

Two large steam elevators are kept constantly busy in the new building.

TELEPHONE SERVICE, ETC.

Another great convenience of the factory is that the various departments are connected by telephone. It is also supplied by the local telephone exchange and a long-distance telephone runs into the main office, so that Mr. Eldredge can as easily talk with New York as with Chicago.

A private wire from the Western Union Telegraph Company runs into the main office and here all the company's messages are received and transmitted by their own special operator. In the bicycle season this is a very important point,

A GLIMPSE INTO THE MAMMOTH DEPARTMENT WHERE BICYCLES ARE ASSEMBLED.
NATIONAL SEWING MACHINE CO.
PHOTO BY CLARK & SOTT.

for then two dozen or more messages are received daily on matters pertaining to the business and requiring immediate attention.

The Company has absolutely left undone nothing that will in any way facilitate the transaction of business and tend to give the greatest satisfaction all around.

Some idea of the amount of business which is annually transacted in the establishment may be gleaned from the fact that it now pays Uncle Sam over $6,000 per year through the Belvidere postoffice for stamps and other postal supplies — one-half the entire receipts of the office.

AS TO ADVERTISING.

The citizens of Belvidere may not realize the fact, but this is one of the best and most thoroughly advertised cities in the United States to-day. For the past nine years the Company has been sending out circulars, pamphlets and catalogues to individuals and firms in every city, town, hamlet and cross-roads in this broad land of ours, not only once, but time and again — a constant stream of advertising matter going out incessantly, making their business more extensively known, winning thousands of new customers and at the same time spreading the fame of Belvidere. In addition to this they advertise at the present time in no less than 1,500 journals of greater or less importance, from the 2x4 sheet in the wilds of Texas to

A SECTION OF THE BICYCLE ENAMELING DEPARTMENT.
NATIONAL SEWING MACHINE CO.
PHOTO BY CLARK & SOTT.

the great metropolitan dailies, including an intermediate list of scores of trade journals and magazines. This broad and extensive system of advertising the Company has not pursued by spells; they have kept everlastingly at it, and are still " pounding away " in this direction, believing that the " constant advertiser is the one who wins the trade." Thus we say that to-day Belvidere is one of the most widely known little cities in the country, and this condition is directly due to the unceasing efforts of the National Sewing Machine Company. To see the beneficial effects we need not look beyond the confines of our own favored city; we need but to visit the factory and look around at the manifold evidences of prosperity within our borders.

The Company has representatives and agents in nearly every town and city in the United States; and not alone in this country is their product known and used — in foreign lands thousands of their sewing machines especially are in use at the present time. They employ constantly three traveling men to look after their interests.

SANITARY FEATURES.

The sanitary features of the factory are as near perfect as it is possible to secure in an establishment of this size. The drainage and ventilation are both excellent, the light is good and plenty of fresh air is always to be had. On every hand, from the tool room to the foundry, from the private offices to the engine room are exemplified order, neatness and cleanliness in matters small and great. These points President Eldredge strenuously insists on being observed by the employes, and are qualities characteristic of the man. He believes in "looking

BICYCLE FRAME AND FILING ROOM IN BICYCLE DEPARTMENT.
NATIONAL SEWING MACHINE CO.
PHOTO BY CLARK & NOTT.

after the little foxes." A walk through the plant (which, by the way, consumes a full half day) will unfold to the visitor one of the most systematic working factories in the world, and show with what religious zeal is the adage, "a place for everything and everything in its place," adhered to by the hundreds of employes.

DIFFERENT DEPARTMENTS.

WHAT THEY ARE, WHO IS THE FOREMAN OF EACH, AND HOW MANY MEN ARE EMPLOYED.

To carry on the business of this factory it requires the co-operation of fifteen separate and distinct departments, as follows:

Department No. 1—Tool. Charles M. Ingalls, foreman; employs 36 men.

Department No. 2—Milling and Drilling. Frank W. Crain, foreman; employs 138 men.

Department No. 3—Shipping. E. E. Manning, foreman; employs 57 men.
Department No. 4—Polishing. L. M. Botsford, foreman; employs 143 men.
Department No. 5—Plating. George M. Elliott, foreman; employs 38 men.
Department No. 6—Press and Stand. H. L. Haywood, foreman; employs 58 men.
Department No. 7—Japan and Enameling. R. H. Jukes, foreman; employs 97 men.
Department No. 8—Sewing Machine Assembling. E. L. Barton, foreman; employs 86 men.
Department No. 9—Screw. W. L. Carpenter, foreman; employs 106 men.

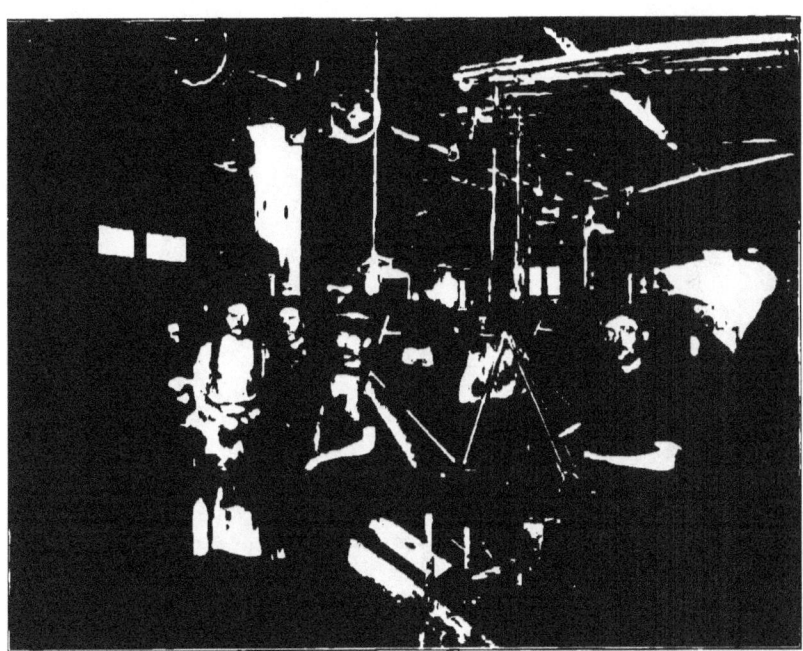

VIEW IN FRAME ROOM OF BICYCLE DEPARTMENT.
NATIONAL SEWING MACHINE CO.
PHOTO BY CLARK & NOTT.

Department No. 10—Stock and Inspection. G. W. Boale, foreman; employs 28 men.
Department 11—Bicycle Assembly. Walter J. Adams, foreman; employs 83 men.
Department No. 12—Attachment and Shuttle. H. Walter Davis, foreman; employs 76 men.
Department No. 13—Bicycle Frame. W. C. Wright, foreman; employs 123 men.
Department No. 14—Foundry. W. H. Moore, superintendent; employs 110 men.
Department No. 15—Chain and Pedal. Employs 59 men.
Department No. 16—Bicycle Enameling. A. H. Arthur, foreman; employs 100 men.

60   BELVIDERE ILLUSTRATED.

This makes a total of 1,338 men employed in these departments. Add to these the 40 office hands and it gives a total of 1,378 persons employed in this busy hive of industry — a city of itself.

IN CONCLUSION.

However much we would desire to give a detailed description of the technical workings of the numerous processes of manufacture in the different departments it is impossible for us to do so us in this space. A general "write-up" is one thing; a comprehensive treatise quite another. To properly describe the countless evolutions through which the many intricate parts used in building sewing machines and bicycles go before coming out the finished product would enlist the greatest

VIEW OF CHAIN AND PEDAL ROOM, BICYCLE DEPARTMENT.
NATIONAL SEWING MACHINE CO.
PHOTO BY CLARK & NOTT.

effort of even a "Philadelphia lawyer," and the subject matter fill a book. The writer is no "Philadelphia lawyer," nor yet a master mechanic. A visit to the plant will be productive of more knowledge in this direction than could ever be gleaned from any written description.

In thus briefly speaking of the National Sewing Machine factory — its past history, its present condition and future prospects — we have adhered strictly to facts, believing that an honest statement of the Company's business and plant as it actually exists to-day were better than all the fulsome praise or wild exaggerations in the world; that it will better subserve the interests of the Company and greater redound to the credit of Belvidere. Tremendous in all its operations little enough can be said in exaltation of this mammoth enterprise. The more one looks into the history of the concern and learns of its methodical, straightforward and thorough manner of doing business the more is one inclined to become lost in enthusiastic admiration of its internecine fabric and workings, and in its completeness recognize the hand of genius, the distinctive impress of great generalship and the certain evidence at every turn of a broad, comprehensive master-mind.

Well may the people of Belvidere be proud of this grand industrial institution and zealously should they guard its every interest. So long as from its towering chimneys rolls the dense smoke — sweet incense to the god of Industry, signifying its prosperous continuation — so long is our city's future thrift assured, so long will our fame throughout the world be known as a great manufacturing center, so long will it be the palladium of Belvidere's commercial success. May its

LOWER FLOOR OF BICYCLE FRAME ENAMELING ROOM.
NATIONAL SEWING MACHINE CO.
PHOTO BY CLARK & NOTT.

shadow never grow less and may its conquests in the sewing machine and bicycle world never cease until "all roads lead to Belvidere."

During the year 1896 several large additions will be built. On May 1 work was begun on a new building which is to be 250 feet by 50 feet and two stories. This will be fire-proof and will be used principally as a stock room. It will cost about $20,000. Besides this a larger, three story, addition will be erected to the enameling building. The Company has just completed a gas plant of its own and is about to build another brick engine house and put in another 400 horse power engine, giving it two engines of that size. This spring the factory has been running night and day to fill orders for both sewing machines and bicycles. Verily, great is the National Sewing Machine Company.

BARNABAS ELDREDGE.

A BRIEF SKETCH OF THIS BUSY MAN'S LIFE AND OF THE EARLY ELDREDGE FAMILY.

We are told that Edward, Zenas and Asael Eldredge came to this country from Wales in their youth and settled at Cape Cod, Mass. How long they remained there is not known. We know that Edward moved to Sharon, N. Y., in after years, while the other brothers sought homes in Connecticut. To the Edward Eldredge branch of the family, and the one of which we shall speak, Barnabas Eldredge, of Belvidere, President of the National Sewing Machine Company, traces his ancestors.

BICYCLE INSPECTION ROOM.
NATIONAL SEWING MACHINE CO.
PHOTO BY CLARK & SOTT.

Edward Eldredge was born September 9, 1737. He died March 28, 1821, in Sharon, Schoharie county, N. Y. He married Adna Hammond in Massachusetts, December 19, 1762. She was born in Dartsmouth, Mass., May 25, 1735, and died in Sharon, N. Y., December 25, 1825. She was one of the family of Hon. Jabez D. Hammond, later the author of "The Political History of New York." Edward and Adna Eldredge had nine children, six sons and three daughters; one son died in infancy. The five brothers at one time all lived on farms adjoining, near Sharon, N. Y. When they separated two of them went to Cortland, N. Y., one to western New York, and two remained at Sharon.

The third son, Barnabas Eldredge, was born September 29, 1768. He died Sharon, N. Y., September 5, 1843. He married Theodosia Wadsworth, soon the Revolutionary war, in Poughkeepsie, N. Y., where she then lived. Sh daughter of Josiah Wadsworth, formerly of Hartford, Conn., where she was born. She died in Sharon, N. Y., May 30, 1831, aged 59 years. In June, 1832, he married his second wife, Sarah Peck. She died April 25, 1873, in Sharon, N. Y., aged 88 years.

Barnabas Eldredge was a member of the general assembly in the state of New York in 1821. His son, Robert Eldredge, was a member of the New York state assembly in 1830, and his son, Seth Eldredge, was a member of the state assembly in 1844.

Barnabas and Theodosia Eldredge had eleven children, viz.: Nancy, Robert, David, Adna, Franklin, Charles, Seth, LeRoy, Sally, Clinton and Betsy.

A SECTION OF THE BICYCLE STORAGE AND CRATING DEPARTMENT.
NATIONAL SEWING MACHINE CO.
PHOTO BY CLARK & NOTT.

Franklin Eldredge was born December 17, 1801, in Sharon, N. Y., the community with which several generations of the family have been prominently identified. November 26, 1822, he married Eliza M. Van Dyke, a descendant of Hedrick Van Dyke, who immigrated to this country from Holland in 1636 — a distinguished character among the early colonists of New York, and the progenitor of an illustrious Knickerbocker family. She was born October 3, 1802, in Middleburg, N. Y., and died August 1, 1879, in Chardon, Ohio. They had twelve children. The eleventh child and youngest son is Barnabas Eldredge, born June 19, 1843, in Munson, Geauga county, Ohio.

Franklin Eldredge settled on a farm in the western reserve of Ohio, and on this farm B. Eldredge was born and brought up. He received his early education in the country schools, and worked on the farm until 1861, when he went to Cleveland to pursue an advanced course of study. Leaving the Cleveland high school shortly before graduation he became connected with the ship-yards of Stephens & Presley as bookkeeper, pursuing at the same time a course of study in a commercial college, from which he graduated.

On August 28, 1865, in Cleveland, Ohio, he married Marie A. Presley, daughter of the junior member of the firm by which he had been employed. They have one son, Franklin P. Eldredge, born January 26, 1867, in Cleveland, Ohio.

Shortly after his marriage Mr. Eldredge engaged in the hardware business in Cleveland as a member of the firm of Van Tassel & Eldredge. It was while engaged in this business that his attention was first attracted to the sewing machine

HOSPITAL DEPARTMENT.
(Very few cases treated each year.)
NATIONAL SEWING MACHINE CO.
PHOTO BY CLARK & NOTT.

trade. He had a brother in Detroit, Mich., who was engaged on an extensive scale in the sale of sewing machines, and in 1866 he became interested with the latter in this business. In 1869 he sold out his hardware business in Cleveland and moved to Detroit to become an active partner in the conduct and management of the sewing machine business. Their trade here extended over a large territory and they had remarkable success in establishing the business of the Domestic Sewing Machine Company, then being introduced into the market. Remaining at Detroit until 1874, Mr. Eldredge then came to Chicago as the general manager of the Domestic Company, having under his control all the territory lying between the western line of Ohio and the Rocky Mountains, and all the Southern States. This position he retained until he turned his attention to the manufacture and sale of his own machine.

Something has already been said of the fierce opposition which he encountered in his attempt to introduce this machine into the market. The most vicious onslaughts were made on him, however, at the very outset of his career as a manufacturer. Infringement suits were brought against him whenever a pretext could be obtained for doing so, and to defend against these suits involved great expense, and led to the serious embarrassment of his business.

In the construction of his machine, he had made use of certain appliances of which rival concerns at once claimed the ownership and control. To establish the fact that their claims were invalid, Mr. Eldredge had to hunt the country over for evidences of the fact that their appliances had been in use before they were patented by the claimants. All over the United States he had agents examining old sewing machines and reporting to him the results of their investigations. In

RESIDENCE OF B. ELDREDGE.
PHOTO BY CLARK & NOTT.

one instance he heard of a machine which he desired to produce in court, it being in the possession of parties who lived in Hamilton, Canada. The information proved to be incorrect, but from clews obtained in Hamilton he traced the machine to Rochester, New York, where he finally gained possession of it, much to his advantage, and won the case in the impending litigation. In another instance while defending a suit brought against him by the Singer Manufacturing Company, he heard of an old machine of which he wished to obtain possession, at Redwood, California. A telegram was sent to San Francisco, and a special agent went out from there to purchase the machine. The agent acted promptly and got hold of it just in time to prevent it passing into the hands of the Singer Company, and with this machine he defeated the latter in the case on trial.

In this spirited and long continued contest Mr. Eldredge showed wonderful persistency, tenacity of purpose and indomitable courage, as well as a vast amount of tact in the conduct of his affairs. These were the qualities most essential to his success at that time, but when he had weathered these storms, and was left free to give his attention to the development of the industry with which he was and still is, so conspicuously identified, it at once became apparent that he had executive ability of a high order and was eminently fitted for carrying forward the work on hand. The subsequent success of the enterprise testifies more strongly than can anything else to the skill and ability with which he has conducted its affairs.

In the management and building up of the bicycle business Mr. Eldredge has exhibited the same progressiveness, the same ability of organization and excellent judgment that has marked his business career from the first. He has boldly entered the field and accomplished in an almost incredibly short space of time, in the face of sharpest competition, what it has taken others years to perform, and what no other man or men ever before did in the same length of time in the same line of trade. This in itself speaks more for his capability and business faculty than all else that we might write. And in this very particular is one of the leading characteristics of Mr. Eldredge's personality manifest—he modestly disclaims any special honor in having made his business the great success it now is, and seeks no fame in this direction.

As Grant was great in war, as Blaine was great in politics, so is Mr. Eldredge great in the commercial world—a born leader. Though energetic and progressive in the highest degree he is likewise cautious and conservative—just the man for the responsible position he occupies. In his comprehension and treatment of all questions and matters of business he is broad-gauged and broad-minded, a man of the greatest acumen and wonderful executive capacity. Honorable in all things, of strictest integrity, approachable and socially agreeable, he commands the respect and esteem of his business colleagues, employes and fellow-citizens, and stands today a living example of what heroic determination and fortitude may do when coupled with brains and a fixedness of purpose. And through all these years of toil and planning, of ceaseless endeavor and accomplishment, Mr. Eldredge has come to know and realize that "nothing succeeds like success," and the quickest and only way to do a thing is to do it.

THE OTHER OFFICERS.
SOMETHING ABOUT VICE-PRESIDENT ELDREDGE AND SECRETARY PATTON.

Without more than a passing mention of the other officers of the Company—the gentlemen above referred to—this article would be woefully incomplete, as their identification with the industry has been and is of such a nature that they form a part of its very life-blood, and are important factors in all its dealings.

Vice-President F. P. Eldredge, the son of President Eldredge, was born in Cleveland, Ohio, January 26, 1867. His early life was spent in that city and in Detroit, Michigan, where his father was engaged in business. There he passed through the trials of youth. In 1874 he moved with his parents to Chicago and there received his early schooling at the Harvard school. He completed his education at the Harvard law school in Boston, from which he graduated in 1887. In January, 1888, he came to Belvidere to reside permanently and to take an active interest in the affairs of the National Company. Upon the reorganization of the Company in 1890 he was elected vice-president, and the wisdom of this choice has been repeatedly shown, for he has proven himself equal to any and all demands made upon him, even under the most trying circumstances. With a zeal born of patriotic enthusiasm he has acquired a complete knowledge of every nook, corner and turn in this great plant and possesses an understanding of its every division and infinite detail that is little short of amazing. No feature of the business within or without the factory is there but that he has familiarized himself with and has it at his tongue's end. Next to his father his opinion, judgment, sanction and advice is most sought. He is the counterpart of his father in all of his traits, characteristics and in manner of doing business. No higher compliment can be paid him than that simple statement. He is finely educated, versatile, brilliant and withal a "prince of good fellows"—one of the salt of the earth. Though young in years Mr. Eldredge carries an old business head, and his capabilities of execution in this direction are only measured by the requirements that may be made upon him. Mr. Eldredge is a prominent Mason, a Mystic Shriner and a member of Medinah Temple, Chicago, and also of the Harvard club, of the same city.

Secretary David Patton was born in Glasslough, near Belfast, Ireland, February 8, 1861. With his parents he came to this country in 1868 and settled in Chicago, where he received his early education in the high schools. Until coming to Belvidere in 1889 nearly his whole life had been spent in that city. He has been associated with B. Eldredge in the sewing machine business continually since 1876 —nearly twenty years—and has been indefatigable in his efforts in building up the business of the National Sewing Machine Company to its present proportions. He is fiancially interested in the enterprise and no man connected with it is more zealous in looking after the "main chance," or exhibits greater fidelity in all matters concerning it than does Secretary Patton. His years of experience in the sewing machine business, gained through his association with Mr. Eldredge, and in particular regarding the affairs of this Company, make him an invaluable adjunct to its successful conduct—indispensable would better express it, for he literally has the details of the business, inside and out, from A to Z, within his grasp. In his present capacity this wide knowledge is of the greatest value and assistance to him in the performance of his duties, and they are many. Like the Messrs. Eldredge he is most emphatically the man for the important position he occupies. Mr. Patton is an advanced Mason, a member of the Knights of Pythias and Royal Arcanum, and socially a "hale fellow well met."

AN IMPORTANT INDUSTRY.

What is now an important industry and bids fair to become a still larger one, is the Cleaveland Spring Bed and Mattress Company. It is next in importance to the big plant of the National Sewing Machine Company. Although President E. A. Cleaveland has been manufacturing spring beds in Belvidere since 1881, the present concern is a new one, the plant having been erected and the company

E. A. CLEAVELAND.

organized by Mr. Cleaveland in 1890. It has a capital stock of $15,000, fully paid, and its officers are as follows: E. A. Cleaveland, president; A. C. Fassett, vice-president; J. W. Sharp, secretary, and A. E. Loop, treasurer. Vice-president Fassett is the county's efficient circuit clerk; Treasurer Loop is cashier of the First National Bank, while Secretary Sharp is a leading grocery dealer.

The factory is thoroughly equipped with all the expensive and intricate machinery necessary for the work. It is operated by steam power, and an average of twenty-five workmen are given employment. The product consists of coil spring beds, woven wire mattresses, cots and children's cribs, and the concern turns out some of the most acceptable, popular and rapidly selling goods now on the markets of the country. Mr. Cleaveland has just invented a new and novel device which does away with many complications in folding cots and cribs. A small invention, yet it promises to greatly enlarge the business, as it is much more simple in construction than any other, more easily operated, and much neater in design. The factory has a capacity of 200 beds per day, and a great many different styles are manufactured. Competent judges affirm that the Cleaveland Spring Bed and Mattress Company turn out the finest line of goods on the market to-day.

Mr. Cleaveland has a long and highly creditable record as a manufacturer. Born in Livingston county, New York, in 1850, he came to Boone county in 1866, and has been a resident of Belvidere seventeen years. He belongs to that class of men known as city-builders, and his coming to Belvidere was a fortunate circumstance, since, with others, he placed his shoulder to the wheel and roused the city from its state of lethargy to the present phenomenal prosperity. He served four years as alderman at the time that the city water-works were completed, and also

CLEAVELAND SPRING BED FACTORY.
PHOTO BY W. H. ROBINSON.

the same length of time on the board of education. He has ever been one of the city's most enterprising and pushing business men. His real estate interests are large. Much credit should be given to Mr. Cleaveland, and the efficient board of directors of the company, for the careful way in which the business has been managed, for it must be taken into consideration that the company was organized and commenced business at the time that the financial troubles were just beginning, and while other factories all over the country were being closed the Cleaveland Spring Bed and Mattress Company never shut down a day and met every obligation promptly. This could never have been done only by careful management. And while the company does not boast of doing as large a business as others who have a much larger working capital it is doing a steady, safe business, and its share toward the prosperity and welfare of the city of Belvidere.

GENERAL ALLEN C. FULLER.

General Allen C. Fuller was born at Farmingham, Conn., September 22, A.D. 1822. His father's name was Lucius Fuller and his mother's maiden name was Candace Newell, and both families were of New England blood. Both parents were for many years among our old settlers, having come to this country in 1845, and both died several years since in this city. Lucius Fuller was for a short time in the mercantile business; was at one time associate judge of the County court, and afterwards postmaster of Belvidere. Our early settlers will remember this aged couple as among the most highly respected and public spirited citizens.

General Fuller was educated in Towanda, Pa. After graduating at the Towanda academy he was placed under the instructions of a thoroughly educated private instructor, and under whom he completed the full course of collegiate study. In 1841 he commenced his law studies, and completed the same at Warsaw, N. Y., in the office of the United States Senator Doolittle, in 1846, when he was admitted to the Supreme court of New York, and in November of that year (1846) arrived at Belvidere, where he has resided since that time, now nearly fifty years.

Within a few days after coming to this city General Fuller was employed in several important cases, and entered upon the active duties of his profession. At this time our population was about 800, and there were but two attorneys here in active practice, Gen. S. A. Hurlbut and W. T. Burgess. Soon after the firms of "Fuller & Burgess" and "Loop & Hurlbut" were formed. These firms continued for several years and did a large business. Between these firms it was "Greek against Greek," and they not only had the business of this county, but were extensively employed in litigation in neighboring counties and the Supreme court.

Devoting himself entirely to his profession for many years, refusing to seek office or participating in party intrigues, and with an iron constitution and indomitable will, he secured and held a large and profitable practice for many years. This was the commencement of his subsequent financial success.

General Fuller has in later years held the following offices: Master in chancery, appraiser of damages on Illinois and Michigan canal, state bank commissioner, county judge, circuit judge, adjutant general of the state, representative and speaker of the house, senator and president pro tem of the senate.

On his return home from public to private life in 1869, our "Old Reliable Belvidere Standard," whose editor had intimately known him for many years, published its opinion of Gen. Fuller, and we copy from its columns the following article:

"For more than eighteen years the name of Allen C. Fuller has been intimately and most favorably known to the people of this portion of the state. In 1846 he came to this place a young, briefless and penniless lawyer. His scholarly attainments, his legal acquirements and his industry and inflexible resolution to succeed, soon brought to him an extensive and lucrative practice, and during the succeeding twelve or fifteen years, while he was in active practice, we presume that no man ever doubted that he ably, zealously and faithfully discharged his duties to his clients. Though always public spirited and liberal, he has, by personal economy and business talent, acquired a handsome property and has contributed much to the growth and prosperity of our town.

"When the war broke out in 1861, General Fuller was then presiding judge of this circuit, and we believe it was universally admitted that he discharged its honorable and responsible duties satisfactorily and with ability. In the summer of that year he was urged by our state officers to connect himself with the military affairs of our state. The bar of the circuit unanimously objected to his resignation, but urged him temporarily to accept the appointment tendered to him of

GENERAL ALLEN C. FULLER.

adjutant general. In the fall of 1861 he entered upon the discharge of the duties of that laborious and exacting and responsible office, and in July, 1862, resigned the office of circuit judge.

"The history and result of his labors during the past three years and a half as adjutant general of the state are too well known to the country to need to be mentioned here. If the opinion of the press, without distinction of party, we believe; if the testimony of Governor Yates, with whom he has been so long associated; if the public opinion, so far as we have heard it expressed, are to be relied upon, then, indeed, he has rendered the state and country capable, faithful and acceptable service. The published reports of the operations of the adjutant general's department in the organizing and sending to the field over two hundred thousand men are before us, and we would wish no better record than to have been so honorably identified with the glorious history of Illinois during this war. Governor Yates in his last message repeats what he has stated in other messages and says: 'General Fuller has been a most able, faithful and energetic officer, and is entitled to the gratitude of the state.'

"The house of representatives, at its last session, unanimously adopted a report of its committee appointed to inspect the adjutant general's office, and from which report we extract the following:

"'That we have thoroughly examined the office of the adjutant general and find it a model of completeness, one that preserves in all its glory the proud record of all our soldiery and reflects infinite credit upon the great state whose sons they are.

"'That in the judgment of this committee the thanks of every patriotic citizen of the state are due to General Fuller for the able and efficient manner in which he has discharged the duties of the office and for his indefatigable efforts in collecting and preserving this glorious record of a glorious state.'

"On the first day of January last General Fuller resigned his office as adjutant general, and having been previously elected a member of the general assembly he was nominated by acclamation by our party, and on the second of January was elected speaker of the house of representatives.

"The manner in which he acquitted himself in this new position may be seen by the following resolution which was unanimously adopted by that body just before the adjournment on the 16th ult:

"'*Resolved*, That we tender our heartfelt thanks to the Hon. Allen C. Fuller, our presiding officer, for the kind, courteous, able and impartial manner in which he has presided over us, and as such recognize in his general bearing and demeanor the perfect model of a gentleman.'

"As a speaker of the house of representatives, and while presiding officer of the senate, General Fuller was, of course, prevented from actively participating in the debates, but we notice from the official proceedings that on the subject of private legislation and the industrial university bill he joins the discussions, and we think our readers will agree with us that in the following extracts from his speeches, which we publish to-day, his views were sound and were ably presented.

"In conclusion we regret to say that General Fuller returns home with his health seriously impaired, but it may be some consolation to him to know that for his long and faithful service he has acquired a high character as a public officer, and enjoys the universal confidence of his old neighbors and friends among whom he has resided so many years."

At this distant day the people of the state may have forgotten, but it is nevertheless true, that they owe General Fuller their lasting gratitude for his service in introducing into the legislature various bills which became laws, among which are the following:

Railroad bills asserting the power and sovereignty of the state to control these corporations in fixing rates upon transporting passengers and freight. His was the first square and honest fight made in this or any other state to fix maximum rates, and the legislation upon this subject was taken to the Supreme court of the state and the Supreme court of the United States, and finally the legal questions of the constitutionality of such laws was sustained by these high tribunals.

Also the law establishing railroad commissions and now in force.

Also establishing a board of public charities and now in force.

Also a bill upon the subject of eminent domain.

Also the revenue law, now substantially in force, was prepared by him.

And the impress of his genius and ability is found on many a page of the Revised Statutes of the State still in force.

Since the close of the war several histories have been written upon our state affairs, and particularly concerning our soldiers and the public men of the state.

Among others may be found "Illinois and the War," two volumes by Eddy, published in 1866; "History of Illinois," by Davidson and Stuve, published in 1874; "Politics and Politicians of Illinois," by D. W. Lusk, published in 1884; "Illinois, Historical and Statistical," two volumes by John Moses, published in 1892.

By a reference to those histories and others it will be found, we believe without exception, that the most unqualified endorsement and approval has been given to General Fuller for the conspicuous part he took in public matters during those times. Though well and favorably known to the bar and business men of Northern Illinois prior to 1860, it was at this time and subsequent years he established a state reputation and maintained the same until he retired from public life in 1872. In

RESIDENCE OF GENERAL ALLEN C. FULLER.
PHOTO BY CLARK & NOTT.

the memorable political contest of 1860 Governor Yates and General Fuller canvassed almost the entire state in behalf of the Republican party, and if we may judge of that canvass, by the opinions of the press of the state as given at that time, it was a most successful and brilliant one, and contributed its full share to the success of the Republican party.

It was not, however, until the late terrible war commenced in 1861, and he assumed the duties of adjutant general of the state, that his name became familiar as household words in every family in the state and especially to our volunteer soldiers. It was in this important office with all its labors, cares, difficulties and responsibilities that he made his most distinctive mark and displayed those rare executive abilities which were admitted by every one. The repeated messages of Governor Yates—the resolutions of our state legislature, and the reports of the federal authorities, as well as the above quoted histories of those years are so entirely unanimous on this subject, that no other opinion need be given in this brief sketch.

After a residence in Belvidere of nearly half a century it can be truly said that General Fuller has established and maintained a character above reproach or question. His word is as good as his bond and all know his bond, if any one could get it, would be unquestionably good. He is believed to have acquired a large fortune and he deserves it. Commencing active life here he still retains the strongest attachment for this city, where his early struggles for success commenced.

In early days here everybody was poor. With no rich or powerful friends to aid in the start, he has, by his indomitable will, his conservative and prudent busi-

GENERAL ALLEN C. FULLER'S PRIVATE OFFICE.
PHOTO BY CLARK & NOTT.

ness management and tireless energy, succeeded in life. His liberality and public spirit here are proverbial. None more so. His gift to this city as hereinafter mentioned proves this and it is now believed that he has made provisions for other worthy public objects. As an evidence of the confidence placed in him as a business man, it may be here stated that he has prominently assisted in establishing half a dozen or more National banks and has held and now holds prominent offices in several of them.

In this brief biographical sketch it is, of course, impossible to do full justice to the reputation and career of a gentleman whose history is part of the history of this great state, and so closely interwoven therewith as to form an essential part of nearly every portion thereof for a period of nearly half a century of progress and achievement. The older citizens who have known and admired him for all these years will not forget, while life shall last, his splendid record and noble character.

They have known him as a citizen and friend; they have respected him for his high character; they have been grateful for his many acts for the benefit and improvement of the city and county of his residence, and they have delighted to honor him with positions of public trust when opportunity offered. His liberal donation of $5,000.00 for the Ida public library, which he founded in honor of his deceased daughter, and which has become one of the finest public libraries in the

SUMMER RESIDENCE OF GENERAL ALLEN C. FULLER.
BAYFIELD, WIS.

state, outside the large cities, was only one of the acts of public benevolence which has endeared him to all classes.

General Fuller, like all great lawyers, has been a great worker. He was always faithful to his client, and gave to every case he undertook, the best efforts of which he was capable. But he surpassed most other men in executive ability which he possessed in a large degree.

This sometimes gave the appearance of austerity to his character, and he has been charged with being overbearing, austere, and unapproachable. Save in the trying days of the nation, when all his great abilities were centered on his country's welfare alone, these charges were without foundation; and then these characteristics were justified by the needs of the hour, when men of blood and iron were necessary to the salvation of the nation. At other times no more genial, companionable and kind hearted man ever breathed. Like the great hero, Grant, in war his nerves were of steel, in peace his heart was tender as a child's, and his sympathies broad enough to embrace all mankind.

His grief over the deaths of his children, whom he idolized, softened, though it did not break him, and he has continued to this day, the capable, active, broadminded man of affairs. When his work shall have been completed and the history of his life written, then will all know that a giant oak has fallen, that a man fit and capable to have ruled over a state or nation has left the impress of his life and achievements upon the community.

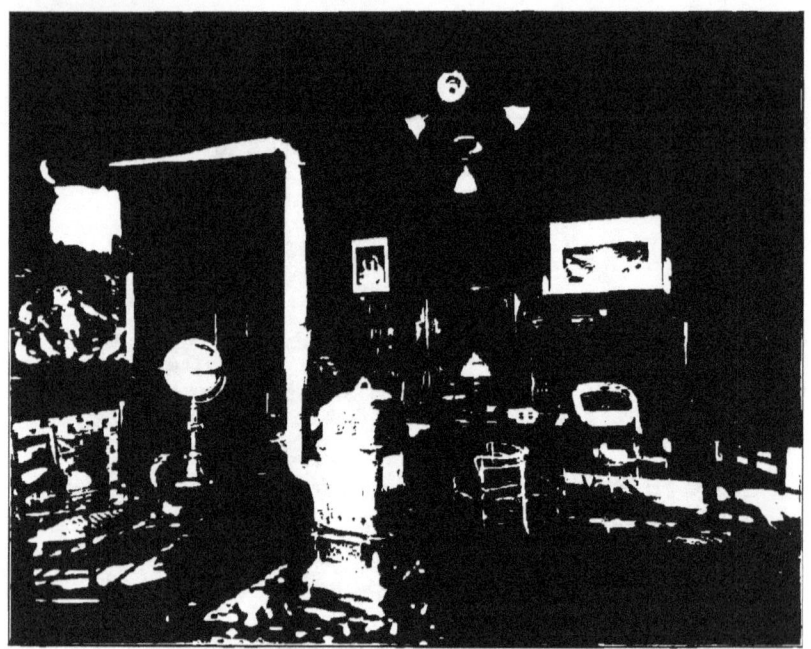

BUSINESS OFFICE OF GENERAL ALLEN C. FULLER.
PHOTO BY CLARK & NOTT.

As yet his eyes are not dimmed, and his strength has not failed. Daily he can be found at his office, where all having business to transact with him can find a cordial greeting and a cheerful readiness to take up and dispose of the business in hand. His business habits and methods are methodical; he familarizes himself fully with every detail of the business in which he may be engaged, and never shirks a duty. His affairs are always in shape, every detail is attended to with scrupulous exactness, and to these qualities is largely due his success in life, in a material way.

Whatever he does is well done, and whatever anyone else to whom he may entrust any matter to do must also be done well, and his employes always are made to realize that their employer always knows at every step of the work whether or not it is done as it should be.

Perhaps this sketch cannot be better closed than by saying that after preparation of the foregoing article the publisher of this book called upo' tinguished member of the bar of this city and one of the most eloquent men of this state, and whose professional and official life for many years enables him to know more than most men, the opinions of the public concerning men of affairs, and requested him to give his impartial and candid opinion of the subject of this sketch.

This is his reply: "Yes, I will do so with pleasure."

"A learned historian of this state has said that 'the history of Illinois could not be written with the name of Allen C. Fuller left out.' Truer words were never spoken, nor a more deserved tribute ever paid to a public servant. In the county of Boone, where he is best known, and where the greater portion of his life has been spent, the name of General Fuller is a household word, and is a synonym for honor, integrity and fair dealing, as well as for worth and ability. Whether at home or abroad, in private or public life, no man ever questioned his honor and integrity; no man ever doubted his public spirit, his broadmindedness or his absolute justice in all his dealings with his fellow men. As a young man, in the practice of law, he was industrious and faithful, and those qualities, coupled with strict honesty and fair ability, could not fail to bring success. He has held the offices of master in chancery, county judge, circuit judge, representative in the general assembly, and speaker of the house, state senator from his district and president of the senate, and adjutant general of the state of Illinois, during the days that 'tried men's souls,' when more than two hundred thousand men went out from Illinois to do battle for the union. In all these positions of trust and honor he acquitted himself with signal ability and with manly honor. No man will deny and none can gainsay that he has been a just and upright judge, a faithful public servant and an honest man in all the relations of life. And such is and will be the final judgment as to his abilities, worth and character."

HON. JOHN J. FOOTE.

John J. Foote was born at Hamilton, N. Y., February 11, 1816. He was a son of John Foote, a distinguished counselor-at-law, and Mary B. Johnson, the daughter of a prominent physician. His genealogy is traced with accuracy to Nathaniel Foote, who emigrated from Colchester, England, and whose name appears on the Massachusetts Bay Colony records of 1633. The descendants of this more immediate ancestor, some of whom are mentioned in Revolutionary annals, long remained in the coast colonies of Massachusetts and Connecticut. After completing his studies in the common schools and Hamilton Academy, and receiving the degree of A. M., conferred by Madison, now Colgate University, he qualified as a druggist, and entered upon and conducted an extensive business in his native town. At the outset of his career, and along its course, the two conspicuous elements of his character were integrity and sincerity, and to these were joined ability and energy. Recognizing the truth of this analysis his friends, added with the years and widening intercourse, made him the repository of important political and financial trusts. After filling with credit a number of local offices, including that of chairman of the Madison county board of supervisors for two years, he was, in 1857, elected senator for Madison, Chenango and Courtland counties, and served his constituency with distinction. In politics Whig and afterward Republican, Mr. Foote has been an earnest champion of the principles advocated by Henry Clay and the great leaders of later times. Among his colleagues in the senate were many who have since become eminent, notably William A. Wheeler, afterward vice-president of the United States. During the session of this first republican legislature, he introduced the "Personal Liberty" bill, an act enlarging the rights of negroes, and other important measures. Mr.

Foote was chairman of the committee on militia, and a member of the banking committee. Mr. Wheeler, chairman of the latter, having been elected president of the senate *pro tem.*, on his motion Mr. Foote succeeded him in the former position. This expression of confidence was valuable, as the committee had great financial responsibility by reason of the panic then impending. In 1860 his name was placed on the Lincoln ticket as an elector for the counties of Madison and Oswego. His acquaintance and association with the leading statesmen of that period was extended, and his co-workers were such men as Governor Morgan, Thurlow Weed, Mayor Opdyke and others of like prominence. Immediately after Fort Sumter had been fired upon the leading men of the state, alarmed at

HON. JOHN J. FOOTE.

the situation, gathered at the Astor House, New York city, for the purpose of considering what steps the commonwealth should take for general protection. Prompt decision was necessary, as the legislature then in session would adjourn within thirty six hours. As a result of the hurried deliberations Mr. Foote was delegated to proceed to Albany, and urge that the motion to adjourn be reconsidered, with view of taking some action relative to placing the state on a war footing. His recommendation was adopted by the legislature, together with the additional suggestion that a bill be immediately passed appropriating three million dollars for military purposes. In 1865, his health failing, and feeling unequal to the demands of official position and business affairs, he removed from Hamilton to his farm near Belvidere. In 1873 he was called to New York city by Ex-Postmaster-General Thomas L. James, an old-time friend, then postmaster, and consented to temporarily accept the position of auditor and acting postmaster, in the absence of his chief, with the object of radically reforming and reorganizing the financial departments of the office. The task before him was herculean, and required for its proper accomplishment a man of ability, courage and fidelity. But the work was in the end satisfactorily completed, and the system adopted became a model for the principal cities of the country. Returning to Belvidere, Mr. Foote has passed the intervening years in caring for his estate, with occasional services of a public nature, particularly as chairman of the board of supervisors for several terms, and in an advisory capacity as director of the First National Bank since 1885. At the home on Lincoln avenue, below illustrated, Mr. Foote lives in retire

RESIDENCE OF JOHN J. FOOTE.

ment with his estimable wife and daughter, Miss Harriet, honored and esteemed by the entire community. John C. Foote, his son, follows his father's earlier occupation of druggist in this city, and a daughter, Mrs. Enos Clark, resides in St. Louis.

SENATOR CHARLES E. FULLER

Was born in Boone county and all his life has resided in this community. His family came to Illinois in 1845, and consequently were among the early settlers. His ancestors were also among the earliest settlers of New England. Dr. Samuel Fuller and his brother Edward came over in the Mayflower in 1620. The immediate ancestor of Charles E. was Robert Fuller, who was born in England and came to this country in the ship Bevis in 1638. He lived first in Salem and afterwards in Rehoboth, Mass. He was the first and only bricklayer in New England for many years. In 1676 the Indians attacked Rehoboth and burned the houses of the settlement. Robert Fuller, having lost his wife and two sons, killed by the

Indians, and his home having been burned, returned to Salem, where he remained until 1696, when he returned to Rehoboth, where he died on May 10, 1706. His oldest son was Jonathan Fuller, born at Salem about 1640, and who married Elizabeth Wilmarth, and resided at Attleboro, Mass. Jonathan had a son, David, born September 11, 1667, who resided at Attleboro, Mass., and Coventry, Conn. He married Mary Ormsby, and they had a son, Elijah Fuller, born September 24, 1724, and who married Mary Wellington, December 8, 1747. They resided in Coventry, Conn., and afterwards in Shaftsbury, Vt. They had a son, Solomon

EX-SENATOR CHAS. E. FULLER.
PHOTO BY CLARK & SON.

Fuller, born March 12, 1757, and his son, Seymour Fuller, born at Shaftsbury, Vt., July 8, 1817, is the father of Charles E. The family have been prominent in New England history since the settlement of this country, and the ancestral heads of the family have generally been men of means and of high character. They were prominently connected with the early colonial wars and several of them lost their lives in King Phillip's war in 1676. From an old historical work we make the following extract as indicative of the opinion generally held of the family:

"The Fuller families were of strong puritanical character; marked for integrity, industry, a strict regard for truth and justice, accompanied by an affability of manners, both pleasing and of controlling influence."

Charles E. Fuller received his education in the common schools of this county, and whatever of success he has achieved in life has been by his own unaided efforts. He read law, first with Hon. O. H. Wright, and afterwards with Hon. Jesse S. Hildrup. He was admitted to the bar in 1870 and has since practiced his profession at Belvidere. He held the office of Corporation Attorney for the old town of Belvidere, before it became a city, for two terms. In 1876 he was elected state's attorney. In 1878 he was elected to the state senate, after a contest which has become historical. He served in the senate for four years, being chairman of the railroad committee and a member of the judiciary and other important committees. He was afterwards elected to the house of representatives three times in succession, where he was a recognized leader, being generally recognized as the party leader and honored by his associates with the chairmanship of the party managing committee. He was also chairman of the house railroad committee. In 1888 he was again elected to the senate, and at the close of his term in 1892 declined a reëlection, preferring to give his time and attention to his large law practice. Mr. Fuller has enjoyed the personal, as well as political, friendship of such men as General John A. Logan, General Richard J. Oglesby, Senator Shelby M. Cullom, Governors John M. Hamilton and Joseph W. Fifer, as well as most of the other political leaders of the state for the past twenty-five years, and has had their entire confidence and respect. In the legislature his friendships were not limited to his party associates, but many of his warmest admirers were to be found on the other side of the house. His opponents admired his abilities, respected him as a man, and had a wholesome regard for his fighting qualities.

Hon. John R. Tanner is authority for the statement that in a political contest on the floor of the legislature Senator Fuller was the readiest debater, the most resourceful parliamentarian and the best fighter he ever knew.

General John C. Black once remarked of him, that he was "one of the few men who always knew how to do the right thing at the right time and in the right way."

In the great senatorial contest of 1885 in the Illinois legislature, when General John A. Logan was reëlected to the United States senate after a contest lasting four months, and in which Mr. Fuller was the Logan leader, he performed services for his party and state, which were afterwards recognized by General Logan in the following letter:

SPRINGFIELD, Ill., May 22, 1885.

HON. CHAS. E. FULLER,

My Dear Friend:—I have relied much upon you as a leader in the late senatorial struggle, and desire now to express my thanks to you and assure you of my appreciation of your untiring labors to achieve a victory for the republican party and myself.

Your brilliant leadership has been most effective in forcing rights from a tyrannical and unscrupulous enemy. The party and myself are under many obligations. Be assured of my life-long regard and friendship.

Very truly yours,
JOHN A. LOGAN.

Mr. Fuller was equally the friend of General Oglesby, and in the senatorial contest of 1891 was chairman of the joint caucus of the house and senate, chairman of the joint steering committee, and manager of the republican side of the contest. The failure to elect General Oglesby or any other republican, was not his fault, but resulted from the independent or F. M. B. A. members, who held the balance of power, going over bodily to the democrats and voting for General Palmer.

Mr. Fuller has expressed the determination to not again be a candidate for any office, but to give his undivided attention to the practice of his profession in which he has been quite successful. He still has a natural liking for politics, however, and generally attends the party conventions of the district and state, where he has been a prominent figure for many years. But he says that he does not expect or desire to again hold any public office himself.

Mr. Fuller was married in 1874 to Miss Sadie Mackey, daughter of Hugh Mackey, of Cherry Valley. They have a pleasant home at 916 South State street.

While in the legislature Mr. Fuller's skill as politician won him a high reputation which was enhanced by his statecraft. In conventions, both state and national, he has shown himself to be a skillful and resourceful politician, and the press of Chicago and throughout the state has several times termed him a party Warwick.

As a legislator Mr. Fuller won recognition as one who believed in legislating for the many, and a number of important bills for the benefit of the masses became laws through his work. While he was potent for his party's good in all conflicts with the opposition, he at the same time rendered valuable service to the people. Zealous for his party and faithful to the people, he left the legislature with an enviable record. In the thirty-fourth general assembly he was virtually speaker of the house, as successor to Mr. Haines, occupying the chair during that portion of the session when, after the senatorial struggle had ended victoriously for the republicans through his efforts, the real legislative work was done. He would have been chosen speaker but for his own advice in opposition to any change in the organization of the house. Mr. Fuller is frequently mentioned in connection with higher honors, and should he reconsider his decision to "leave politics alone and practice law," he will surely be heard from. Mr. Fuller is a natural orator and his eloquent voice has been heard in all parts of the state. On the stump he is what is known as a magnetic man. He is considered to be one of the best stump speakers in the state and his services are always in demand by the party committees.

As a citizen of Belvidere Mr. Fuller has been prominent as well as in the field of public affairs. His energetic, progressive spirit has had much to do with the upbuilding of Belvidere. Successful in law, politics and business affairs, distinguished as an orator and legislator, popular at home and abroad, and an associate of the leading men of Illinois, the pride which the people of Belvidere and Boone county take in him is pardonable indeed.

WILLIAM C. DE WOLF, JR.

Is a native of the soil, having been born in the town of Spring, in Boone county, on the 4th day of November, 1865. As a boy he worked on his father's farm, and attended the district school at the old stone school house at Shattuck's grove. Later he attended the high school at Genoa, De Kalb county, where he graduated in 1885. He afterward read law in the office of Judge C. B. Dean, and was admitted to practice by the Supreme Court of the state in 1887. Later in the same year he entered into a co-partnership with Hon. Charles E. Fuller in the practice of the law and has continued to be so associated with Mr. Fuller to the present time. The firm is one of the strongest and enjoys a practice said to be quite lucrative, and which is not by any means limited to the county of Boone, but extends into the adjoining counties as well. Mr. DeWolf has given his attention almost exclusively to the practice of his profession, and has not generally given much of his time to political matters, although he is a staunch and active Republican, and is generally a delegate to the party conventions. He is a member of the district republican senatorial committee. He was once appointed and twice elected city attorney of Belvidere, but resigned the office in 1891 and has since declined to be a candidate. Mr. De Wolf's associates at the bar all have the greatest respect for his character and abilities. He has an eminently judicial cast of mind, is studious and well read and always absolutely fair and honest. Mr. De Wolf is married and has one child. One who knows him intimately when

W. C. DeWOLF, Jr.
PHOTO BY YOUNDT.

asked to give an estimate of his character said: "Mr. De Wolf is a man of whom one's opinion improves with acquaintance. The better you know him the greater will be your admiration of his character and sterling qualities. He is a man you can tie to. If he is your friend you can count on him in sunshine and in storm. There need be no doubt as to where he stands. He is perfectly reliable; absolutely true. He never betrayed a trust and never will. He is a good judge of character and knows how to choose his friends. He is a positive man, with a clear, incisive, vigorous mind, and consequently a good lawyer."

HON. R. W. WRIGHT.

Robert W. Wright, the present efficient state's attorney was born in Belvidere, July 19, 1862. He attended the public schools and at the age of 16 began the study of law in his father's law office. On the completion of a course at the Illinois University at Champaign he was admitted to the bar in January, 1883, being only twenty-one years of age at the time. He was chosen state's attorney by the people of this county at the November election of 1884—a signal honor for one

R. W. WRIGHT,
State's Attorney.
PHOTO BY YOUNDT.

of his age. He has been re-elected at the end of each succeeding term since that date. His marriage to Miss Ida Osborn, of Champaign, took place March 11, 1885. Mr. Wright met the young lady while attending the University. They have one child, a Miss now ten years of age. Mr. Wright rose rapidly to the front as a lawyer and commanded a lucrative practice. In 1894 he was appointed corporation counsel for the city of Belvidere, which position he still holds. His advancement and continued endorsement from the people of this city and county, afford abundant evidence that his talents receive the most genuine recognition that a community could possibly give. Admitted to possess very much more than the ordinary qualifications demanded in a practitioner and legal representative of the people's interests, the county and city wisely retain his services. Mr. Wright is a forcible and brilliant speaker, and has the reputation of conducting to a successful issue the cases falling to his charge, to a degree not always attained by older representatives at the bar. His practice is not confined to this city, but includes many other of the important centers in Northern Illinois, and especially Chicago, where he is called frequently. As a counselor, pleader and official, Mr. Wright has, by sheer ability and application, as well as personal popularity, taken and maintained a position in the very front ranks of the legal fraternity of the state. He is a shrewd and brainy lawyer—a lawyer worthy of the name. He has

RESIDENCE OF R. W. WRIGHT.
PHOTO BY CLARK & NOTT.

no desire to mix in state or national politics, but his sole ambition is as a lawyer. In the new era pertaining to the progress of Belvidere the services of Mr. Wright have been of exceeding value, and fully appreciated by the community.

JUDGE W. W. WOOD.

Judge Wales W. Wood was born in Hinsdale, Cattaraugus county, New York, April 25, 1837, and is a son of Col. Emery Wood, who, while a boy, served in the war of 1812, and was afterward colonel of a New York state militia regiment. Judge Wood, at the age of sixteen, was sent to the Genesee Wesleyan College at Lima, N. Y., where he entered freshman year, full classical course, remaining there two years, and completing his college course, graduated with honors at Union College, Schenectady, N. Y., under Dr. Nott, in the year 1857. Out of his class, numbering over one hundred, he was one of the twelve selected by the faculty of that college to the Honorary Society of "Phi Beta Kappa." In the fall of that year he came West, located at Belvidere, and read law with the then well-known law firm of Fuller & Wood, being the present Gen. A. C. Fuller, of this city, and Hon. Wm. H. Wood, now of Chicago. In 1860 he was admitted to the bar, and practiced his profession here until the summer of 1862, when, upon the president's call for more volunteers to put down the rebellion, he enlisted in Company G, 95th regiment, Illinois Volunteer Infantry, and upon the muster-in of the regiment, Sep-

WALES W. WOOD.
COUNTY JUDGE.

tember 4, 1862, at Rockford, Ill., was promoted, and commissioned by Governor Yates as adjutant of that regiment. He acted in that capacity with his regiment in the field throughout General Grant's campaign in northern Mississippi, in the fall of 1862, and in the spring of 1863, while the army was in camp at Lake Providence, La., he was chosen to perform the duties of assistant adjutant general, by Gen. John McArthur, of the 6th Division, 17th Army Corps, Army of the Tennessee, took active part in the following campaign and siege of Vicksburg, and after the surrender served as post adjutant of that city under Gen. McArthur. He was in the battles at Nashville, Tenn., December 15 and 16, 1864, when the Union army commanded by General Thomas met and routed the Confederate forces under Hood, and in the siege and taking of Spanish Fort and Mobile, Ala., in the early part of 1865. He remained on similar duty until near the close of the war, when he re-joined, and was mustered out with his regiment at Camp Butler, Springfield, Ill., in August, 1865. At the close of the war he returned to Belvidere, and resumed the practice of law, and about that time wrote and published a history of the 95th regiment. In 1866 he was married to Miss Alice E. Humphrey, and they have one daughter, Gertrude C. Wood. Soon after returning, resuming his profession, he was appointed master in chancery of the circuit court of Boone county, holding that office some eight years, and subsequently was corporation and city attorney for Belvidere, and also states attorney of Boone county for several terms. In the spring of 1889 he was elected county judge of this county, since which time he has been continued in that office. Judge Wood is a prominent member of Hurlbut Post, G. A. R., of this city, having been commander of that post, and held other offices in the organization. The fact that Judge Wood is so frequently called to Chicago to hold court is evidence that his decisions are regarded as fair and impartial. As a judge he is a credit to the bench.

NORTH STATE STREET RESIDENCE PORTION.
LOOKING NORTH.

EX-JUDGE C. B. DEAN.

The name of C. B. Dean occupies a prominent place in the history of Belvidere and Boone county. He has always taken an active interest in public affairs. He was born in Franklin, De Kalb county. His father came west from Maine in the early days, and when horses were scarce in California he and his son made several overland trips with herds of equines destined for sale in the California market. It required four months in which to make a trip.

Judge Dean located at Belvidere in 1862. For a short time he was employed in E. W. Case's grocery store. Then taking up the study of law and entering the Ann Arbor (Mich.) law school, he graduated in the class of 1873. He was married at Ann Arbor, and went to Denver to practice law. He returned to Belvidere one year later, and soon took rank among the leading attorneys. He was city attorney for several terms, and was elected county judge three successive terms, for which office he was eminently fitted. His wife's health failing in 1888, he resigned from the bench and removed to Talapoosa, Ga., where he remained about four years, after which the family moved back to Belvidere. Mr. Dean has the only set of abstract books in Boone county, which are quite valuable and are increasing in value as the county grows older and people become more careful of their titles. Judge Dean was one of the most enthusiastic workers in the movement which brought to Belvidere the great National Sewing Machine Company. He was one of the negotiating committee and spent time and money to secure the prize. He did not accept stock for his subscription, but contributed with a loyal, patriotic purpose. This one incident gives a key to his character. If Belvidere had more like him it would be better for the city.

Mr. Dean is now practicing law. He is an able lawyer and is therefore very successful. He is a Republican in politics and is chairman of the county republican committee.

WILLIAM L. PIERCE.

Well advanced on the list of prominent Belvidere attorneys is the name of William L. Pierce. A son of William H. and Mary J. Pierce, he was born in the town of Spring, June 3, 1868. After a thorough preparatory course of study in the best schools of the county he entered the Northwestern Law College, from which he graduated June 16, 1892. Beginning practice immediately thereafter, in partnership with F. J. Evans, in this city, the association was continued until business demands necessitated a dissolution. He was married to Miss Laura M. Duth, of Freeport, Ill., October 31, 1895. Fluent, versatile, clear in statement, and a valuable counselor, Mr. Pierce commands the attention of juries and the confidence of the public. A number of important cases here and elsewhere conducted by Mr. Pierce to a successful issue, adorn a record which might well be contemplated with satisfaction. His practice in this and adjoining counties is extended and growing, and a very bright future awaits this talented member of the bar.

FRANK S. WHITMAN, M. D.

The name of ex-Mayor F. S. Whitman is closely linked with the growth and enterprise of Belvidere. He was born in this city September 27, 1849, and is a descendant of good old New England stock. Both his grandfather and father located in this city in early days and were leading factors in the pioneer history of Boone county. His father, Hiram, came here from Chautauqua county, N. Y., in 1839, making the entire distance overland with teams.

Dr. Whitman has the honor of being the second oldest practitioner in Belvidere. After acquiring his early education from the public schools he became a student at the Chicago University and subsequently engaged in teaching one year, being principal of the Roscoe school. He began the study of medicine with Dr. James K. Soule, of Belvidere, and graduated from the Hahnemann Medical College, of Chicago, in February, 1872. The same year he opened an office in this city and has since successfully engaged in practice. His skill and marked ability have placed him at the head of the list.

Dr. Whitman's name is synonymous with progression. He is regarded as one of the best "posted" men in Belvidere. He is one of the first to push along any project calculated to advance the interests of the city. He has always had great faith in the future of Belvidere, and by shrewd and careful real estate investments has acquired a competence. He never allows these outside matters, however, to interfere with his professional duties. Last summer he erected a splendid business block in which are his offices and which are equipped in a modern manner. The

DR. F. S. WHITMAN.
PHOTO BY YOUNDT.

doctor is a large stockholder in the National Sewing Machine Co., and was one of the founders of the People's bank, of which he is vice-president. He is also interested in other enterprises.

Politically he is a staunch Republican and is one of the leaders of the party in this congressional district. He is a member of the congressional committee for this district, and was an alternate delegate-at-large at the National convention of 1892. When it comes to careful political judgment the doctor has few equals. Locally, he has had high public honors thrust upon him. He has served as president of the school board, alderman, mayor for two successive terms, three terms as coroner and was president of the Boone county board of pension examiners for a number of years.

Impaired health, the result of a too constant application to professional duties for nearly a quarter of a century, and the desire for a share of the leisure enjoyed by other men, and never obtainable in the work allotted him, were causes that led the doctor to announce on April 1st last his retirement from the active conduct of his profession. His future work is to be closely confined to the line of consultation.

A. W. SWIFT, M. D.

No young physician has gained distinction more rapidly than Dr. A. W. Swift, who has been associated with Dr. F. S. Whitman for ten years. He was born in Nunda, Livingstone county, New York, in 1860, and

DR. A. W. SWIFT.
PHOTO BY YOUNDT.

came to Belvidere when but five years old. His father was one of the brave defenders of the stars and stripes and laid down his life in the cause of liberty on a southern battlefield.

In early life the doctor chose the medical profession and studied with Dr. Whitman. He subsequently attended the Chicago Homeopathic Medical College and graduated with honors in the class of 1885. Forming a partnership with Dr. Whitman he soon established himself as a skillful physician and won the confidence of the people. He has been a practitioner here for ten years and no physician stands higher in public esteem. In 1885 he married Miss Jessie Curtis, daughter of Charles Curtis, one of the early settlers of Boone county. He has

DR. D. E. FOOTE.
PHOTO BY CLARK & NOTT.

been a member of the board of education and is at present a member of the board of health and a member of the official board of the Methodist Episcopal church. He has never been a seeker of public office but prefers to devote his entire time and attention to the practice of medicine. He owes his success in his profession largely to his hard, conscientious work, and his example is a good one for young physicians to emulate. He is popular socially and has a still brighter future before him.

DANIEL E. FOOTE, M.D.

Dr. Foote was a native of Chenango county, New York. His ancestors were English, and loyal to their country and king, as indicated by the Foote coat-of-arms which is in his possession, having been handed down to him in the regular order of inheritance. It has upon its chevron "Name of Foote," and beneath, upon a scroll, the words "Loyalty and Truth." The doctor traces his lineage in an unbroken line from Nathaniel Foote, one of the first settlers of Wethersfield, Conn., whose successors were prominent in the colonial wars and the war of the revolution. He is a member of the Society of the Sons of the Revolution for the state of Illinois. Dr. Foote is a graduate of the University of Buffalo's medical department, and received his diploma from the hand of Millard Fillmore, chancellor of the university while president of the United States. His preceptor was Frederick Hyde, M.D., late professor of surgery and dean of the faculty in the medical college of Syracuse, N. Y., with whom he studied medicine and surgery five years, and then practiced one year. He practiced his profession at Newark Valley, Tioga county, New York, two years, where, in 1853, he married Martha E. Updegraff. In 1854 they removed to Belvidere, where he has since been in constant practice. In 1855 he purchased the place where they now reside, on which, in 1873, he built the house still occupied. They have three daughters, the

RESIDENCE AND OFFICE OF DR. D. E. FOOTE.

eldest of whom is the wife of Edwin W. Warren, of Belvidere, the other two remaining with their parents. Dr. Foote is a permanent member of the American Medical Association and of the Illinois State Medical Society, an elder in the Presbyterian church, and has occupied many places of honor and responsibility, both municipal and social.

DR. R. W. M'INNES.

Dr. R. W. McInnes was elected to the office of mayor at an important period in the history of Belvidere. It was at a time when a strong and safe guiding hand was needed in the administration of our city affairs. The city was indeed fortunate in placing him at the public helm last spring. He is wide-awake to the growing needs of a growing city, is progressive and enterprising in spirit, and is in full sympathy with the many needed improvements already decided upon or now under serious contemplation. Opportunity's hand was stretched forth and Mayor McInnes grasped it with enthusiasm. Among the improvements he has advocated sanitary sewers, water works extension, and paving, and all are likely to come during his term of office. It will be no fault of his if they do not.

Dr. McInnes was born in Rockford in 1857. He attended the public schools there and subsequently took a four years course in Beloit College. He resolved to study medicine and entered Northwestern Medical University, graduating in 1884. Shortly after becoming an M. D., he located in Belvidere, associating himself with Dr. Charles Scott, then the leading physician of Belvidere. At Dr. Scott's death six years later, or in 1890, the extensive practice naturally largely reverted to Dr. McInnes, who had attained an enviable prominence in the profession. Dr. McInnes deserves the honors which have been bestowed upon him. He lives in a

DR. R. W. McINNES,
MAYOR.

pretty residence on North State street. He and his estimable wife are popular in Belvidere's society circles.

A. J. MARKLEY, M. D.

Dr. A. J. Markley has practiced medicine in Boone county for nearly fifteen years. He first located in Poplar Grove, where he remained one year. Then he moved to Garden Prairie, and lived at that village for eight years. In 1890 he came to Belvidere, forming a partnership with Dr. R. W. McInnes. The doctor was born in Archbald, Fulton county, Ohio, May 3, 1858. He graduated from the Bennont Medical College, Chicago, in the class of 1881, and no member of his class has been more successful in the medical world.

Dr. Markley congratulates himself that he located in so progressive a city as Belvidere, and Belvidere reciprocates the sentiment. In his profession he has proved himself worthy of the highest confidence, and as a citizen has won the esteem of all.

He chose for his wife a Boone county girl, who was living in Fairbury, Neb., at the time of their marriage, in 1887. She was Miss Belle B. Bills, whose parents were early residents of Bonus. Dr. and Mrs. Markley live on South State

DR. A. J. MARKLEY.
PHOTO BY YOUNDT.

RESIDENCE OF DR. A. J. MARKLEY.
PHOTO BY CLARK & NOTT.

street, in one of the costliest and most beautiful residences in Belvidere. Their friends are legion.

Dr. Markley has taken an active interest in school matters, and has served as president of the South Belvidere school board. Much credit is due him and his co-laborers on the board for the excellent school whose destinies they guide.

CHARLES DARWIN CARPENTER, M. D.

Dr. Carpenter, while only recently taking up his residence in Belvidere, is yet a practitioner of diversified experience, and eminently qualified to assume and maintain a leading position in the fraternity of this city. The doctor gravitated

DR. CHAS. DARWIN CARPENTER.

naturally into the profession of medicine; his father and preceptor, George H. Carpenter, M. D., at one time surgeon of the 91st Ohio Volunteer Infantry, in the late war, being a prominent physician of Athens, Ohio. His mother, Mary Welch, was a daughter of the Hon. John Welch, late chief justice of Ohio. The subject of this sketch was born in Athens, Dec. 12, 1849, and received his classical education at the Ohio University. Graduating from the Ohio Medical College at Cincinnati, March 1, 1872, he began practice with his father in the home vicinage, but was finally attracted to Cleveland, where he remained a number of years discharging the manifold duties entailed by an extensive practice. He was also one of the resident physicians at the Columbus, Ohio, Hospital for the Insane during the years 1877-78. Dr. Carpenter is president of the pension examining board at Belvidere. He was married to Miss Rena Vlereborne, January 26, 1882. They have two interesting daughters, one of three and the other ten years of age. The family reside on Logan avenue. Dr. Carpenter's skill, culture and varied talents, together with his social qualities, are bringing him friends in his adopted city, whose promise led to a choice of what he hopes to make his permanent home.

R. H. BURTON, M.D.

It is not an exaggeration to say that no young physician and surgeon has achieved success to a more marked degree than Dr. R. H. Burton. Although his practice here dates only over a period of two years, he is already recognized as one of the leading physicians. He was born in Toronto, Canada, in 1861. His father, John C. Burton, settled south of Belvidere in 1879, and was a prosperous

DR. R. H. BURTON.
PHOTO BY CLARK & NOTT.

farmer. He died in 1895. The doctor's home has been in Belvidere for years, and when he opened an office here he felt that he was not among strangers.

Dr. Burton attended the Northwestern University for a time, and then went into the drug business in Chicago, being in that line for eight years. He subsequently became a student at the Chicago College of Physicians and Surgeons, from which institution he graduated with credit to himself and the class of which he was a member. He took an interneship in Alexian Brothers' famous hospital and one also in St. Elizabeth hospital, being directly under the preceptorship of that eminent surgeon, Dr. J. B. Murphy. The doctor's extended hospital experience has been of incalculable value to him in his practice. He has been especially successful in performing delicate and dangerous surgical operations, and in these his hospital training comes into good use. Before coming to Belvidere he practiced one year in Chicago.

IRVING J. HECKMAN, M.D.

Was born in the township of Kingston, De Kalb county, twelve miles southeast of Belvidere, September 16, 1861. His father, Philip Heckman, of German ancestry, soon after his marriage, early in the '50's, removed from Ohio to this vicinity. His mother, Sarah A. Heckman, was of Scotch and English descent, and one of a large family. Both were of the sturdy and reliant type of pioneers, and readily adapted themselves to the new situation. The doctor received his primary education in the schools of De Kalb county and Belvidere, and attended college at Hillsdale, Mich. After following the avocations usually engaged in by young men of high aspirations, but indefinite purpose, he finally entered the

DR. I. J. HECKMAN.

Illinois College of Pharmacy at Chicago, and subsequent to the completion of his studies filled the position of dispenser in the Elgin Hospital for the Insane under the Fifer administration. In 1891 Dr. Heckman was married to Miss Carrie Hewitt, of Chicago, a native of Winnebago county and a graduate of Rockford College. In 1895 he graduated from the College of Physicians and Surgeons, of Chicago, and settled in Belvidere, where he has already taken a prominent place among the successful practitioners of the city.

CHARLES SCOTT, M.D.

Dr. Charles Scott, now deceased, was in more respects than one a remarkable man. He was for years the leading physician of Belvidere, and was loved by the people as few men have been. Large-hearted, sympathetic, helpful, and of fine abilities, he lived in the esteem and confidence of all with whom he came in con-

DR. CHAS. SCOTT, (Deceased).
PHOTO BY YOUNDT.

tact. He was the son of Dr. Amos Scott, who is still living at the old homestead in Seward, Winnebago county. His ancestors on his father's side were Pennsylvania Dutch, and of Quaker affiliation. On his mother's side they were Scotch Irish from the north of Ireland. Dr. Scott was born May 26, 1849, in Washington, Penn. He came with his father's family to Illinois in 1857. His early education was obtained at the public schools, including a course at the Pecatonica High School. Before taking up the study of medicine he worked his father's farm while the latter was a surgeon in the army. He studied medicine at Chicago Medical College during the winters of 1872-3 and 1873-4, and was at Rush Medical College in 1874-5, graduating in 1875. After discharging the duties of interne at St. Luke's Hospital, he came to Belvidere in 1876. In May, 1877, he was married to Miss Clara E. Tousley. The doctor achieved phenomenal success in his profession. He arrived in Belvidere financially indebted, as he had been obliged to work his way through college, but with the result which often follows unaided and persistent effort. His mental equipment was of so complete a nature that the time was not long postponed when every hour had urgent demand. At the height of usefulness and on the crest of success, the effects of overwork became rapid-

RESIDENCE OF MRS. DR. SCOTT.

ly apparent, and the skillful physician and faithful friend, widely known and trusted, sank to his last sleep, sincerely mourned by the entire community. His death occurred in this city July 25, 1890. Mrs. Scott still resides, with her two children, Charles R. and Clara May, in the beautiful home erected by the doctor not long before his decease. The son Charles, if his inclination be followed, will take up the study of a profession of which his father was a shining ornament.

WILLIS BUTTERFIELD, A.M., M.D.

Dr. Butterfield was born in 1848, and has practiced medicine since 1872, coming to Belvidere in 1885. His immediate ancestors date from New Hampshire,

DR. WILLIS BUTTERFIELD.
PHOTO BY YOUNDT.

and his great grandfather and grandfather participated in two of the earlier wars — the former as major of a regiment from that state in the revolutionary conflict, and latter as captain in the campaigns of 1812. His father, who is now in Denver, Col., came to Illinois in 1846. The doctor was educated at the Northwestern University, and afterward for a year was principal of a graded school at Byron, Ill. On graduation from the medical department of the university named, at a later date he located in Iowa, where, at De Witt and the Hospital for the Insane at Independence, he discharged the ordinary and special duties of his profession. From there he transferred his allegiance to Barrington, Cook county, Illinois, at which place he remained ten years working hard in a large and successful practice. During his residence there he occupied the position of surgeon for the Chicago and Northwestern Railroad Company, and was also at one time a company surgeon of the Denver and Rio Grande Railroad in Colorado. Dr. Butterfield was married to Miss Grace Wells in 1879. They have three young daughters.

A. C. FASSETT.

A. C. Fassett, circuit clerk and recorder, is one of the most popular men in Boone county. In giving a sketch of him in "Belvidere Illustrated" this can truthfully be said. He is essentially a man of the people, and such men are always well liked. Mr. Fassett was born in Hartwick, Otsego county, New York, in 1845. He located at Garden Prairie, in this county, in 1875, and conducted a general store there in partnership with J. D. Rosekrans for nine years. He was elected circuit clerk and recorder in 1884, and is now in his third term. In public

A. C. FASSETT,
CIRCUIT CLERK.
PHOTO BY YOUNDT.

office the people love to find a plain man and one who is courteous and accommodating. Mr. Fassett is all this and more.

He enlisted with the Sixteenth New York Battery when the war broke out, and served with distinction. He went in as a private, and his bravery and merit won him promotions to second lieutenant. Mr. Fassett was in many hard-fought engagements, but did the hardest fighting at Fredericksburg and at Fort Harris, near Richmond. He has been elected commander of Hurlbut Post, G. A. R., for nine consecutive years, and venerable counsel of the M. W. A. for eight successive years. He is one of the prominent members of the Methodist church, being clerk of the board of trustees and clerk of the official board. He has been superintendent of the Sunday-school, and was for five years president of the County Sunday-school Association. He is president of the Board of Education of North Belvidere, having served in that capacity for six years; is president of the Board of

Trustees of the Campmeeting Association, and is a member of the Public Library Board. Mrs. Fassett's maiden name was Miss A. S. Hopkins, and the couple were married at Edmeston in 1866. Their only son, Will, is a railway postal clerk, running between Chicago and Dubuque.

WM. BOWLEY, COUNTY CLERK.

Wm. Bowley, although a young man, holds one of the most responsible official positions within the gift of the people of Boone county. He was honored a year ago by being elected county clerk and he has proved himself worthy in every way of the trust reposed in him. Mr. Bowley was born in Boone county thirty-three

WILLIAM BOWLEY,
COUNTY CLERK,
PHOTO BY CLARK & NOTT.

years ago. His father was among the pioneer settlers of this section and was a loved and respected citizen.

The subject of this sketch received a thorough education in the public schools and at the age of eighteen years began his business career in the dry goods trade. Beginning with a small start, he made heroic and successful strides towards success when the fire-fiend destroyed his store and ruined him financially.

That the people of Belvidere and Boone county have full confidence in Mr. Bowley was grandly demonstrated when he entered the race for county clerk. His opponent was C. M. Keeler, whom it was considered impossible to defeat. The campaign was a memorable one, in fact the most exciting the county has known in years. Mr. Bowley made a splendid canvass of the entire county and conducted his campaign like a veteran. His magnificent work won for him a great victory, and he was nominated and elected by a safe majority. Since assuming the duties of the office he has done the work satisfactorily and well. He is genial and accommodating and every possible courtesy is shown to the public. The books and records were never kept in better shape, all of which proves the people made the right choice.

Six years ago Mr. Bowley married Miss Ida Miller, daughter of Isaac Miller, a well-to-do citizen who was held in high esteem. Mrs. Bowley is an artistic milliner and conducts fine millinery parlors which are popular with the ladies.

The general opinion is that County Clerk Bowley is slated for more and continued honors, and he deserves them.

ALD. W. H. MOORE.
PHOTO BY YOUNDT.

ALDERMAN W. H. MOORE.

W. H. Moore is one of the most active members of the city council. He was first elected alderman in 1892, serving two years, during which time he demonstrated marked ability in the administration of city affairs. He retired from the council for one year, and in the spring of 1895 the people of his ward insisted on his taking the office again, and he was elected without opposition. Mr. Moore's services to the city are valuable. He is foremost in advocating needed reforms and improvements. He heartily supported the ordinance providing for a complete sanitary sewer system which passed the council, and the next advanced step he championed was a paid fire department, which the city badly needed. As chairman of the fire and water committee, he was in a position to bring about just such a reform.

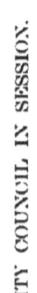

CITY COUNCIL IN SESSION.
PHOTO BY CLARK & MOTT.

Mr. Moore came to Belvidere from Chicago in 1886, when the June manufacturing Company moved to this city. In point of continuous service, he is the oldest employe of the National Sewing Machine Company. Identifying himself with the concern seventeen years ago, he has worked in every department, and the ramifications of the sewing machine business are all familiar to him. For some years he was shipping clerk and now holds the responsible position of superintendent of the foundry having nearly one hundred and thirty men under his charge.

In the Masonic order Mr. Moore is prominent. He is a thirty-second degree mason, being a member of the Freeport Consistory. He is also a member of

Tebala Temple Mystic Shrine, and Crusader Commandery, Knights Templar of Rockford. Mr. Moore is popular with all classes.

He lives in a handsome dwelling on East Lincoln avenue which he recently built and fitted with electric lights and all modern improvements.

ALDERMAN F. H. DIXON,

Contractor and builder, stands in the very front rank of Belvidere's artisans. He was born in Oneida county, New York state, in 1861, and came to Illinois in 1866, locating in Boone county. Learning the carpenter's trade at an early age he has continuously followed it and its higher branches for a period of sixteen years.

ALD. F. H. DIXON.
PHOTO BY CLARK & NOTT.

His work as contractor and builder is the product of the last eight years. Perhaps the most important undertaking in his later experience was that of superintending the construction of the National Sewing Machine Company's new building, erected during the past season at a cost of $100,000. This was a charge of great responsibility, involving much study of detail, and constant watchfulness. Very many of the fine public edifices and costly private residences adorning Belvidere are the result of his careful planning and supervision. The South Side school building No. 1, the shoe factory, Whitman and Starr's buildings, Kuppler's handsome block, the National's foundry and milling department, the latter completed about three years ago, and scores of dwellings ranging from the cottage to the mansion, are testimonials of his ability and thorough methods. Mr. Dixon was chosen alderman from the first ward at the spring election of last year, and his practical knowledge enables him to render valuable service in the council and on committees.

ALD. B. F. HARNISH.

B. F. Harnish is what might be called a self-made man. Sixteen years ago he came to Belvidere from York, Pa., where his parents reside. He began as messenger boy for the Western Union and Chicago & Northwestern Companies, at the same time turning his attention to telegraphy. He was gradually promoted to the positions of night operator, day operator and finally chief clerk at the local station. In the last named capacity he rendered fourteen years of efficient service. Two years ago he accepted the position of assistant cashier of the People's Bank, and the fact that such a responsible position was tendered him is alone sufficient evidence of the

ALD. B. F. HARNISH.

high place he holds among his fellows. He has served as city treasurer and is now in his second year as alderman. At such an important period in the history of Belvidere it is well that so progressive a citizen as Alderman Harnish is connected with municipal administration. He is greatly interested in the work of fraternal and benevolent societies, and is a member of the Masonic chapter, Knights of Pythias, Royal Arcanum and Red Men.

Mr. Harnish was born thirty-seven years ago near Lancaster, Pa. In 1888 he married Miss Nellie Hayes, daughter of A. Hayes. They have one son. The friends of Alderman Harnish are numbered by legions and that deservedly.

EX-ALD. FRANK KING.
PHOTO BY YOUNDT.

FRED J. EVANS.

Mr. Evans, the present city attorney, was born in this county in 1869. His father, John Evans, and grandfather, Samuel Evans, came to Boone county from Otsego county, N. Y., in the pioneer days of this section. After finishing a complete high school course in 1886, Mr. Evans engaged in business, and remained therein until 1891, when he entered the law department of the Northwestern University. His graduation was soon followed by a law partnership with W. L. Pierce, and the firm existed until April, 1893. At the spring election of the latter

FRED. J. EVANS,
CITY ATTORNEY.
PHOTO BY CLARK & NOTT.

year he was chosen by the people to represent them in the position he now occupies. Excellent service and superior qualifications ensured his selection for a second term, which began last year. In addition to his general practice as an attorney, Mr. Evans devotes a considerable portion of his time to real estate, insurance and loans, and his clientage is numerous and increasing. His convenient offices are in the Hotel Evans, of which he is the proprietor. His marriage to Miss Kate B. Lewis of this city, took place August 4, 1892. They have one child a bright little daughter about three years of age, and an attractive home on Locust street. To his energy and progressive methods, coupled with unquestioned reliability, may be attributed the enviable position he occupies in the community, and his popularity with all classes.

C. M. CHURCH.

C. M. Church, druggist and county treasurer, was born in McHenry county, Ill., and accompanied his parents to Bonus, Boone county, at an early age. He received a common school education, and turned his attention to the drug business, commencing work in Belvidere with J. C. Saxton one of the earlier pharmacists. He has been identified with the same line up to the present time. In August, 1890, he opened a drug store on State street where by careful and conservative business principles and integrity in all his dealings, he succeeded in building up a

C. M. CHURCH,
COUNTY TREASURER.

trade that necessitated removal to more extensive quarters. In November, 1894, he changed his location to March & Petitt's new block on Logan avenue, and opened one of the best pharmacies in the city. His efforts to furnish reliable qualities to his customers is being rewarded by a constantly increasing patronage. Seldom do druggists aspire to public office, but Mr. Church is an exception to the rule. He holds the responsible position of county treasurer having been elected one year ago. At the primaries Mr. Church was pitted against some strong opponents but was chosen by a large majority. Thus far he has given the utmost satisfaction and by his personal attention to the details of the work will doubtless prove a reliable and competent official.

JOHN W. SHARP.

Numbered among the leading men of Belvidere is John W. Sharp. Mr. Sharp is a leader because he takes an active interest in public affairs, and is among the citizens who are striving to upbuild the city. He is the proprietor of one of the largest grocery stores in Belvidere and his is a successful business. He served two years as alderman and has just been reëlected. His record in the city council was commendable. He is now serving his second term as supervisor, and is poormaster of the city. In this capacity much important charitable work is under his direction. He has a big heart and no deserving person is turned away. Mr. Sharp is also a member of the North Belvidere Board of Education and feels a pardonable pride in the $25,000 school building just erected under the supervision of the board. He is a prominent member of the M. E. church, being one of the stewards and also treasurer. Mr. Sharp is a man of high integrity, business-like in business affairs,

ALD. J. W. SHARP.
PHOTO BY YOUNDT.

and affable socially. In public matters he looks scrupulously after the interests of his constituents.

He was born in Lake county, Ohio, in 1855. His parents moved to Livingstone county, Illinois, in 1867, and he located in Belvidere eight years ago. He and his family live in a comfortable home on West Lincoln avenue. Mr. Sharp thinks Belvidere is destined to enjoy a greater growth than it has in the past.

LEVI ROBERT FITZER.

Levi Robert Fitzer, county superintendent of schools, was born in the town of LeRoy, in this county, September 7, 1864. His ancestors on his father's side came to this country during the early part of the eighteenth century and settled in the states of New Jersey and Pennsylvania, one branch of the family having come from Germany and another from England. Some of their descendants served with the Continental forces in the Revolutionary War, and by virtue of this service, L. R. Fitzer is a member of the society, "Sons of the Revolution." His father, Levi F. Fitzer, came to Illinois from Tompkins county, New York, with his parents in the '40's, and settled on a farm near Harvard. In 1862 he married Eliza J. Cummings, was born in Newark, N. J., in 1846, of Scotch-Irish parentage. Later he joined the Ninety-fifth Illinois Volunteer Regiment in the Civil War, and died while in the service in January, 1865. In 1867 his widow and the mother of L. R. Fitzer, was married to J. W. Van Antwerp, and for twenty-five years they lived on a farm near Capron. Here the subject of our sketch spent his boyhood. He completed the common school course of study at the Capron public school, and then entered the Illinois State Normal University, graduating there-

L. R. FITZER.
COUNTY SUPERINTENDENT OF SCHOOLS.
PHOTO BY CLARK & NOTT.

from in 1886. Returning home, he engaged in teaching in this county with marked success for a period of three years. Afterwards, he established a newspaper — *The Boone County Banner* — at Capron, and conducted it for nearly two years. The publication was finally disposed of and moved to Belvidere, and in time was succeeded by the *Republican*. In 1890 he was elected to the position now so worthily filled, and re-elected in 1894. His removal to this city in 1892 was occasioned by the necessity of a central location. That the important duties of the office have been discharged with fidelity and ability is evidenced by the popular verdict and by results apparent from conscientious application of later-day methods to educational supervision. Mr. Fitzer was married October 9, 1895, to Miss Louise M. Swail, a daughter of the Hon. William D. Swail, president of the People's Bank of Belvidere. He is one of the stewards of the Methodist Episcopal church, and is an active Sunday-school worker, being at present secretary of the County Association. He is an extensive reader in various lines and is a young man of studious habits, having completed one term's work in the University of Chicago during the past year in addition to his regular official duties.

FLOYD SMITH, SHERIFF OF BOONE COUNTY.

The chief executive officer of this county is now serving his first term. To properly discharge the duties of his position peculiar qualifications are requisite— among them a clear head, cool courage, promptitude in action, good judgment and adequate mental equipment. That these distinguish the present incumbent are evidenced by the fact of his election and the performance of routine and special

FLOYD SMITH,
SHERIFF.

work falling to his charge. Elected in the fall of 1894 after one of the most hotly contested political engagements of record in the county, by the largest majority ever given to a successful candidate. Prior to his election Mr. Smith had been deputy sheriff for four years under his predecessor, so that the requirements of the present office were not unfamiliar. Previously to accepting the former position he had been road commissioner for a period of nine years. Sheriff Smith's father, Samuel Smith, came with his parents to Boone County from Chenango County, New York, at the age of thirteen years, in 1839, and thus has within his memory the pioneer and fruition days of the two extremes. His marriage to Miss Jeneatte Storms occurred in Belvidere. The subject of this sketch was born in this city January 16, 1855, where he has since resided, with the exception of a few years passed in farming, and two years' absence in Chicago shortly after the great fire. He was married to Miss Hattie E. Tucker at Belvidere July 24, 1889. He has one son of eighteen, by a former marriage. The business of the office greatly increases with the development of the city and county, and its responsibilities become more extended. It should be a matter of congratulation to the public that it is filled by a representative citizen entirely worthy the confidence reposed in his reliability and efficiency.

A. E. JENNER.

Asher E. Jenner, second son and fifth child of Stephen and Eliza Jenner, was born in the town of Moriah, N. Y., April 10, 1818. He resided there until 1831, when his parents removed to Chautauqua county, in the same state. April 10, 1832, he went to Jamestown, N. Y., where he learned the jeweler's trade of James

A. E. JENNER,
CITY CLERK.
PHOTO BY CLARK & NOTT.

Harrison, and remained there until the spring of 1838, when he came to Chicago by way of the lakes, and on foot from there to Belvidere, where he arrived June 1, 1838. Here he opened a watch-repairing shop, the first between Chicago and Galena. At that time there were no buildings on what is now the south side, within the present city limits, and but eleven structures on the north side, including two frames without rafters. For the first three or four months he had charge of the post office, where all the postal business of the county was transacted, and knew personally nearly every inhabitant of the county. In 1840 he was married to Mary Jane Cook, who died in 1854, leaving two sons, Charles J., ex-sheriff of Chautauqua county, N. Y., and George C., vice-president of the American Copying Co., of Jamestown, N. Y. In 1856 he was united in marriage to Emmaroy E. Lyon, of Burlington, Vt., to whom two daughters were born, Kittie H., who resides in Chicago, and Nellie A., who died in 1882. He has been engaged in the watch and hardware business, but for the last thirty-five years has devoted himself to official duties. He was elected Town Clerk in 1860, and has been re-elected every year since; was elected Justice of the Peace in 1861, and has held the office continuously since that date; was appointed Corporation Clerk in 1857, and, with the exception of three years, has held this position jointly with that of City Clerk since then. During this period he has held the office of County Treasurer three or four terms, besides being School Commissioner and Clerk of Board of County Commissioners, one term each. These long terms of service testify to the confidence and regard of the public, and his ability to still discharge the duties of official position in an eminently satisfactory manner is still unimpaired.

E. E. SPOONER,
SUPERINTENDENT OF WATER WORKS.
PHOTO BY YOUNDT.

E. E. SPOONER.

In few divisions of public service is a competent man more indispensable as chief than in that of the waterworks department. Belvidere congratulates herself on the fact that the gentleman now filling this position has all the needed requirements, and that his splendid management has given us a system of which every patriotic citizen may well be proud. E. E. Spooner has had charge of the waterworks since the plant was first acquired, having arrived here in January, 1891, to superintend its construction. The excellent results stand as a monument to his ability and skill. Mr. Spooner is a native of Maine. He was born at Bangor, in 1851. In 1857 his parents moved to the west, and settled in Ogle county, Illinois. His experience as a mechanic and engineer extends over a period of nearly a score of years. Practically, his first work was for A. S. Cox, a well-known older resident of Belvidere, whose home was then at Rochelle. Himself and a brother conducted mills for Mr. Cox, both at Rochelle and DeKalb, at the time of the Chicago fire. His next position was with Wesley Stewart & Co., in Lee county, with which firm he remained for nine years. When the citizens of Rochelle decided to put in a waterworks system, they called upon Mr. Spooner to take charge of the construction, and he remained as superintendent for nine years, or until he was engaged by the City of Belvidere. Few men can point to the record of holding but four positions since beginning mechanical and engineering work, but that is nevertheless the memorandum possible to be made by the genial Superintendent. The people of Belvidere hold him high in their esteem and confidence, both as a citizen and an expert. Superintendent Spooner is a member of Belvidere Lodge A. F. & A. M., the Knights of the Globe, and the I. O. O. F.

JOHN THREN,
FIRE MARSHAL.

JOHN THREN.

A half-million cigars is the number manufactured and sold by John Thren in a single year. Mr. Thren has been in the wholesale and retail cigar and tobacco business in Belvidere for ten years. He was born in Chicago thirty-eight years ago, and has the push and hustle characteristic of the Chicagoan. He has conducted the principal cigar and tobacco store of Belvidere for many years. Connoisseurs aver that Mr. Thren's leading ten cent cigar "Solace" is not excelled by any other brand made. Mr. Thren was appointed Chief of Belvidere's fire department in the spring of 1895, and the city never made a better selection of fire marshal. He has great confidence in the future of Belvidere, and recently demonstrated it by investing five thousand dollars in two South State street business lots, on which it his intention to build at an early date.

F. L. GOODRICH.

The National Sewing Machine Company has the good fortune to be supplied with the best talent in every department requiring the oversight of an expert. One of the most important of these positions is that held by F. L. Goodrich, the highly efficient purchasing agent, who associated himself with the big concern about four years ago, coming to this city from Chicago. He is widely known as the inventor and patentee of numerous sewing machine attachments, which are considered superior to anything of a similar nature on the market. These attachments are now being largely manufactured by the National. The "Goodrich" attachments

F. L. GOODRICH.
PURCHASING AGENT NATIONAL SEWING MACHINE CO.
PHOTO BY YOUNDT.

are, by reason of priority of invention and excellence, standard articles, and as familiar to the trade generally as "C" sugar to the grocer. Mr. Goodrich's father was a pioneer in this particular line, which the son took up and developed to its present importance. At the World's Fair the only medal and award given to exhibitors in this line was that for the Goodrich attachments. This affords a final proof of their superiority. Their use on sewing machines is to make possible the perfect execution of fancy work of every kind. In another portion of this work a description of the attachment department is given in detail, and the manufacture of these specialties referred to. Mr. Goodrich has been engaged in manufacturing for eighteen years. He was connected for some time with the Goodrich Manufacturing Company of Chicago as secretary. This concern did a large and profitable business for a number of years. Now permanently identified with Belvidere and its interests, and holding the most important relations with the National Company. Mr. Goodrich is a valuable addition to the business circles of the city, and with his interesting family to its best social element.

HENRY W. AVERY.

This influential citizen was born in Ledyard, Conn., May 31, 1823. The founder of the family emigrated from Salisbury, England, in 1630, and settled at Gloucester, Mass. His father, Henry W. Avery, a soldier of the war of 1812, came to this county in 1854. His elder brother, Rev. F. D. Avery, was pastor of the Congregational church at Columbia, Conn., for forty-five years. The

RESIDENCE OF F. L. GOODRICH.
PEARL STREET.

subject of this sketch left his eastern home for Illinois in 1845, and in Flora township, this county, purchased forty acres of land at a price of $400. This small beginning eventuated in a tract of three hundred acres. In 1881 he moved to Belvidere. Mr. Avery has been twice married—to his first wife in 1844, who died in 1847, and to his present companion, Rachel P. McCord, of Carlisle, Pa., in 1848. His only child, Elizabeth, died in 1880, leaving three sons. In 1842 Mr. Avery joined the Congregational church at Ledyard, and three years later united with the Presbyterian organization of Belvidere. In 1852 he was ordained a ruling elder, and was in 1855 elected clerk of the session, which position he has held continuously, and still occupies. He has also been secretary and treasurer of the society without intermission since 1870, and with but few lapses since 1853. His particular delight and success has been as a Sunday school worker, having been first elected superintendent of the Presbyterian school in 1846, and he has served thirty-two years. He was for ten years president of the Boone County Sunday School Association. An evidence of the general confidence in his ability and integrity may be found in the fact that he has been intrusted with the care and settlement of many estates. He has been secretary of the Belvidere Farmers' Insurance Company for fourteen years, during which time the amount of risks has been increased from $289,387 to $2,045,925. He is president of the Belvidere Cemetery Association, and has also served as assessor, justice of the peace, supervisor and member of the school board. In 1887 the Freeport Presbytery licensed him to preach, and he is frequently called upon to supply vacant pulpits, and con-

H. W. AVERY.
PHOTO BY CLARK & NOTT.

duct or aid on funeral occasions. Mr. Avery is a ready and forcible writer and fluent speaker, and has the esteem and regard of a community that recognizes the value of his public and friendly services.

GEORGE W. MURCH.

This enterprising citizen was born at Courtland, N. Y., January 19, 1830. His parents Martin and Polly Murch, who remained in the state mentioned until 1861, then came to Belvidere, and resided with their son, G. W. Murch, until the time of their decease some years later. In 1849 Mr. Murch forsook the homestead and journeyed to the beckoning west, locating in Putnam county, Illinois, where he addressed himself for about a year to business and teaching. With three other young men, in the spring of 1850, the second year after gold was discovered in California he started for the coast, walking to St. Joseph, Mo., and continuing thence by oxteam across the plains. After 116 days of travel he arrived at his destination and engaged in mining. Returning in 1852 to Putnam county via Panama and New York, he finally settled in Belvidere in 1853. Here he opened a harness shop with his brother, L. H. Adding clothing and boots and shoes a few years later, and building and occupying with the same lines in 1857 a substantial block on the South side which was just beginning to reveal the possibilities of trade, they maintained both stores until 1874. At this time the two stocks were combined, the harness department closed and Mr. G. W. Murch conducted an extensive business alone until 1873 when he retired. He was married to Miss A. L. Amsden at this place in 1857. They have two children, Mrs. J. F. C. Dick, now residing in California, and Mrs. Rev. A. W. Burton, at home. When in 1886 the project of removing the June Sewing Machine Manufactory of Chicago to this city was in the incipient stage, Mr. Murch was appointed chairman of the citizen's

G. W. MURCH.

committee having the matter in charge. The soliciting of subscriptions to stock and donations, as well as other arduous labor, were requisite, and Mr. Murch's tireless efforts were largely instrumental in installing the factory. He was elected vice-president and a director of the original company. The positions of trust filled by Mr. Murch have been numerous, notably those of town trustee, town and city treasurer and member of the board of supervisors, and he has been a director of the People's bank since its organization. Mr. Murch has always been a leading spirit in enterprises of a public nature, active in church and social affairs, and at the front in business undertakings.

W. S. BROWN.

One might search the country over and not find a man more eminently qualified, or one in whom the requirements for the arduous duties of the position are more happily combined, than W. S. Brown, superintendent of the great and growing National Sewing Machine Company. This is a position no ordinary man could fill. Indeed, were its superintendent incompetent, the results would be disastrous. Mr. Brown's connection with the National Company began eight years ago. He came here to accept a subordinate assignment, but upon an early discovery of his worth promotion to the position of master mechanic followed. As time wore on his services became more valuable, and subsequently, when advanced to the superintendency, it was simply a reward of merit—a promotion as deserved as wise on the part of the Company. He is thoroughly practical, and is a genius in many respects. The complete and systematic organization of the different departments of the factory is admirable, and to Superintendent Brown, full measure of credit for his contribution to the general result must be given. W. S. Brown was born in

W. S. BROWN.
SUPERINTENDENT NATIONAL SEWING MACHINE CO.
PHOTO BY YOUNDT.

Kellogsville, Ashtabula county, Ohio, in January, 1855. At various times he held positions with the Geneva and the Noble Sewing Machine companies. He was for four years with electrical manufacturing concerns, two years with the Thomson-Houston Company, of Lynn, Mass., and superintendent for some time of the Mayo Electric Company, of Boston. Mr. Brown has a wife and interesting family. Mrs. Brown is an active member of the Presbyterian church. The Brown domicile on East Lincoln avenue is pleasantly situated, overlooking the river and South Division, and the plant to which all his energies are given.

J. R. BALLIET.

Ranking high among the active business men of Belvidere is the subject of this sketch. He was born in Genoa, DeKalb county, February 26, 1848, his rents John and Hannah Balliet having there located in 1846, when the country was sparsely settled. Having passed his earlier days on the farm, he attended school in Woodstock, McHenry county, Ill., after which he taught a country school in his old neighborhood for three winters. In 1868 his fortunes were cast with the people of this city, where he engaged in the Piano, Organ and Sewing Machine line, and the writing of fire insurance, both of which he still continues, having built up a sound and prosperous business. He was married to Miss Mary L. Detrick, of Belvidere, December 23, 1874. Besides attending to his regular business, Mr. Balliet has found opportunity to devote considerable time to other interests. He assisted in organizing and putting in successful operation the Belvidere Electric Light Company, of which he has been secretary since its beginning.

J. R. BALLIET.
PHOTO BY YOUNDT.

He is also president of the Belvidere Telephone Company, commencing business January 1, 1895, of which he was one of the original promoters. It has now over 250 subscribers. He is a stockholder in the People's bank, and largely interested in the National Sewing Machine Company, of which latter corporation he has been one of the directors since 1889. His fraternal relations are with the Masonic order, of which he is a thirty-second degree member, the American Legion of Honor and the Knights of Pythias. Of genial presence, untiring application and fine abilities, Mr. Balliet stands among the leaders in the social and business circles of the city.

M. G. LEONARD.

M. G. Leonard, now retired, has been identified with the business and commercial interests of Belvidere for nearly half a century. He came here when our city numbered less than one thousand souls. Mr. Leonard was born in Gloversville, N. Y., May 20, 1824. He attended the public schools at that place and St. Johnsville until seventeen years of age, and then entered the military school in

Oswego. On completing the course there he engaged in teaching in Oswego until 1846, when he emigrated west, settling in Belvidere. The first thing he did was to secure forty acres of government land. Railroads were unknown here at that time and all produce was hauled to Chicago. Mr. Leonard embarked in the mercantile business, keeping a general store and continued operations in that line for five years, when he turned his attention to dealing in real estate and handling grain, also doing an insurance and banking business. For forty years he was engaged in buying and shipping grain and for several years dealt in coal and wood. Two years ago he sold out his business to Marshall Bros. He, however, still owns the elevator building and valuable real estate in and around Belvidere. A sad

MARCELLUS G. LEONARD.

event occurred July 22, 1886, when Mr. Leonard's beloved wife passed away. Her maiden name was Mary Root. Two daughters born to them died within two days of each other in 1864. Politically Mr. Leonard is a Republican and has served as alderman and county superintendent of schools. He is one of Belvidere's leading and honored citizens.

GEORGE M. MARSHALL.

Nothing succeeds like success. Among the young business men of Belvidere none have been more successful than George M. Marshall. Mr. Marshall was born on a farm in Sycamore, DeKalb county, Illinois, October 18, 1861, and received his early education in a district school, which he attended until he was sixteen years old, then he attended the Sycamore high school for two years, after which he finished his education by taking a complete course in Chicago Business College, after which he lived in the city one year, acting as city collector for Marshall Field & Co. His father, Thomas Marshall, was one of the early settlers of DeKalb county, and is to-day one of the largest land holders of that county residing at present on one of his farms in Sycamore township. Mr. Marshall has been engaged in the grain business for ten years. Four years ago Mr. Marshall located in Belvidere, and has never regretted that step. He first purchased a half interest in the old established elevator and coal business of M. G. Leonard. Two years ago Mr. Marshall's brother, Taylor Z., bought out Mr. Leonard's interest, and the firm is now Marshall Bros. They run a grain elevator which has a capacity of 40,000 bushels, and have an extensive coal and feed trade. They own the city scales property at the corner of Whitney and Buchanan streets. George Marshall is a young man of great business capacity. His unques-

GEORGE M. MARSHALL.
PHOTO BY CLARK & NOTT.

tioned integrity and uprightness have won for him the esteem of all who know him. In politics Mr. Marshall is a Republican. February 3, 1886, he married Miss Susie S. Cottrell of Sycamore, and three bright and interesting children grace his pleasasant home. They are Florence, Gilbert and Thomas. A few months ago Mr. Marshall became owner of a fine residence on Pearl street, a property worth $5,000. Both Mr. and Mrs. Marshall are active members of the Methodist church. He predicts a flowery future for Belvidere, and pins his faith to this city by branching out in business and investing in real estate.

OLIVER BECKINGTON.

Among the prominent citizens of Boone county Oliver Beckington has long maintained a leading position. He was born in the town of Spring, this county, July 27, 1848. His parents, Thomas B. and Sarah Beckington, came direct to Belvidere from Somerset, England, in 1847, and settled on a farm in Spring township. Oliver Beckington early in life adopted the business of auctioneering, which he has constantly followed for over thirty years, his field of effort being at first in the vicinity of his home and afterwards Chicago. In the year 1869 he went to California, where he remained until 1871. While there he achieved marked success, visiting in the course of business nearly every prominent city in the state, and receiving a medal awarded him as the best salesman among thirty-seven competitors on the coast. Returning to the east he finally established himself in Belvidere, which has since been his home. He was married to Miss Rosa J. Roper, March 25, 1875. They have four children — one son, aged 19, and three daughters. In

O. BECKINGTON,
THE NOTED AUCTIONEER.

the fall of 1886 he made an independent fight for the shrievalty of Boone county, and it was one of the most closely contested on record. His majority was about four to one. The administration of affairs during the four years through which he was an incumbent of the office, was most energetic and capable, and a reëlection would assuredly have followed but for the constitutional limitation. Mr. Beckington's business is still that of auctioneer, real estate, and the buying and selling, as he expresses it, of "anything on earth." As an auctioneer his fame is widespread, and the scope of his operations has extended to every adjacent State. With growing reputation the sales were of a more important character, involving large amounts, and became more like town meetings than ordinary vendues. There probably is not his superior in the successful conduct of sales of consequence in the western states, while his public spirit, energy and open-handedness entitle him to recognition as one of the most valued members of the community.

WILLARD T. LONGCOR.

Belvidere owes her progress and development in different lines, in a large degree, to the push and enterprise of her young men, and among them the name of Willard T. Longcor is conspicuous.

Leonard S. Longcor, father of Willard T., was born here in 1845, and was one of the city's most successful business men as well as one of her best beloved citizens. He was identified in the upbuilding of Belvidere in various ways. The L. S. Longcor business block on North State street was erected by him. He passed away December 5, 1894.

WILLARD T. LONGCOR.

The subject of this sketch was born in this city, August 17, 1872. His boyhood days were passed under auspicious skies, and he was not slow to take advantage of the splendid opportunities which fell to his lot. After taking a course in the public schools and graduating from the North Belvidere High School, he entered Lake Forest University, where he spent two years. Subsequently he became a student at Monmouth College, taking the course of study antecedent to law and journalism. From this institution he was graduated with honors in 1894, the faculty and trustees conferring upon him the degree of Bachelor of Literature. Returning to Belvidere, he assisted his father in business matters, and at the death of his father he assumed the active management of the business left by him.

Mr. Longcor is financially interested in most of Belvidere's enterprises, and is also the holder of a large amount of valuable real estate in the city and surrounding country. He was one of the organizers of the Belvidere Gas Light and Fuel Company, and is secretary of that corporation as well as one of its directors. Mr.

Longcor is shrewd and careful in his business dealings, and by his good financial policy and strict integrity has won the respect of veteran financiers. Socially he is popular with all who know him. He is one of the trustees of the First Presbyterian church, and in politics he is a staunch Republican.

BELVIDERE GAS LIGHT AND FUEL COMPANY.

A gas plant in a city the size of Belvidere is now considered a necessity, and the works of The Belvidere Gas Light and Fuel Company supplies that want. This company was incorporated April 15, 1895, and the works built and completed during the same year. The mains of the company cover thoroughly every part of the city, and consists of a total of eleven miles in actual service. The apparatus

THE BELVIDERE GAS WORKS.

used in making gas is of the famous Gilmore type, the gas being obtained from gas oil which is a refined product of crude oil. The apparatus consists of three generators, the necessary seals, scrubbers, condensers, purifyers, oil and water pumps, steam blowers, etc. The company has one of the finest and largest gas holders west of Chicago, it having a storage capacity of 50,000 cubic feet of gas while the apparatus itself will produce 300,000 cubic feet per day. The oil storage tank has a capacity of 12,000 gallons. In addition to the regular apparatus the company has a station meter of the latest improved pattern at its works which registers the output of the gas from the plant.

Gas when used in connection with the Welsbach Burner produces the finest artificial light known, it being far superior in quality to the incandescent electric and much cheaper, in fact it has been demonstrated in our city again and again that a 60 candle power light as produced with gas through a Welsbach Burner can be had at one-third the cost of a 16 candle power incandescent electric.

As a fuel for cooking and light heating gas has no equal. It is cheaper than coal, wood or gasoline, besides being more convenient, cleanly, safe and reliable.

Gas was first turned into the Company's mains October 11, 1895, and notwithstanding the lateness of the season it secured and is now supplying a large number of consumers with gas for both illuminating and fuel purposes. The output for this year will reach nearly 10,000,000 cubic feet. The stockholders of the company are the following well known business men: F. S. Rowan, Real Estate Dealer, Belvidere; John L. Witbeck, Director First National Bank, Belvidere; W. T. Longcor, Real Estate Dealer, Belvidere; Irving Terwilliger, Cashier Second National Bank, Belvidere; Geo. H. Hurlbut, Ex-Mayor, Belvidere; John H. Witbeck, Vice-President Fort Dearborn National Bank, Chicago; Hon. Wm. J. Henley, Judge of the

JOHN C. LONGCOR.
PHOTO BY YOUNPT.

Appellate Court of Indiana, Rushville, Indiana; Geo. W. Campbell, Atty. at Law, Rushville, Indiana; P. R. Kennedy, Alderman, Belvidere; Hon. Stephen D. May, Atty. at Law, Chicago; Jesse Wheeland, Engineer, C. & N. W. Ry.

JOHN C. LONGCOR.

John C. Longcor was born in Belvidere August 8, 1847. His father, Samuel Longcor, came here in 1840, and was widely known all over the country, from the fact that he was the inventor of the famous "Diamond" plow, which had a large sale. In his boyhood days the subject of this sketch attended the public schools, taking a thorough course in the high school. For some years he was associated with his father in the manufacturing business, and subsequently he became identified with the drug trade. In 1874 he established a drug store on North State street, and since that time he has conducted a highly successful business. He carries one of the largest and most complete stocks in the city, and is regarded as one of the substantial business men who form the backbone of Belvidere.

Mr. Longcor was married February 16, 1881, to Miss Eva M. Barker, who is one of the city's talented and accomplished women. She possesses a fine alto voice, is one of the prominent members of the Ladies' Lyric club and leader of the Methodist choir. Mr. Longcor is affiliated with the M. E. church, being one of the trustees. He is justly popular, and few citizens are more highly esteemed than he. He is fairly well supplied with this world's goods, a competence which he has accumulated by his conservative and careful business policy. He belongs to the A. O. U. W. Mr. and Mrs. Longcor have one of the finest homes in the city on West Lincoln avenue.

RESIDENCE OF FRANK TOUSLEY.

ALD. WILLIAM H. DERTHICK.

Alderman Derthick was born in this city January 18, 1842. His parents, Nelson and Margaret Derthick, came to Belvidere from Richfield Springs, N. Y., in 1837. After receiving a common school education Mr. Derthick, at the outbreak of the rebellion, joined the contingent of ninety-day men sent to Freeport, which was mustered in by General Pope with Company B, Fifteenth Illinois Infantry, May 24, 1861. This was the first regiment of volunteers sworn into the service of the United States for the war. At the surrender of Donelson, engaged at Pittsburg Landing, where he was wounded; afterward at Vicksburg, where he received a gun-shot wound in the knee, and which finally caused his discharge from the service at Jefferson Barracks, St. Louis, in August, 1863, are events in an honorable record. Upon returning to Belvidere he learned the painter's and decorator's trade, and since acquiring it has, without exception, been his own employer. In 1871, during the rebuilding of Chicago, he obtained several large contracts and employed 175 men. Mr. Derthick was the first to engage in artistic decorating west of Chicago, and his reputation is widespread. Churches, schools,

W. H. DERTHICK'S OPERA HOUSE BLOCK.
PHOTO BY CLARK & NOTT.

INTERIOR OF W. H. DERTHICK'S PAINT AND WALL PAPER STORE.
PHOTO BY CLARK & NOTT.

public buildings and residences of every degree illustrate the extent and variety of his work. The last and perhaps crowning effort is the elaborate adorning of the National's superb offices. As a builder Mr. Derthick has been conspicuous, even at a time when returns seemed doubtful, having erected, occupied and sold over thirty-five houses, from the cottage to the mansion. When the June Sewing Machine Manufacturing Company contemplated the transfer of its plant to Belvidere, Alderman Derthick was chosen one of the citizen's committee to negotiate the change and solicit subscriptions. His energetic service contributed largely to the successful issue. Mr. Derthick was elected alderman from the second ward in 1890, and served one term. In 1894 he moved into the fourth ward, and was

W. H. DERTHICK.
PHOTO BY CLARK & NOTT.

chosen to fill the term now being served. Alderman Derthick has been an official of Hurlbut Post, G. A. R., of this city, since its organization. He was married in 1864 to Miss Charlotte Reed, who died in 1878, and on April 21, 1887, to Miss Lizzie Martyn. The children by his first marriage were Harry and Paul, now deceased, and Mrs. Piel and Mrs. Merveaux, of this city, and by the latter union Charlotte, now at the age of six years. One of the side enterprises undertaken by Mr. Derthick is the management of the Opera House, whose stock of $17,000, with the exception of a tenth part, he owns. Large outlays have been made upon this principal place of entertainment, and its productiveness quadrupled. As a progressive, public-spirited, capable citizen and official, Alderman Derthick stands among the first, and his constant and effective services receive high appreciation.

THE BELVIDERE CARPET STRETCHER.

The Belvidere Carpet Stretcher and Tacker was invented by Edward L. McDivitt, of this city, and he was awarded patent February 21, 1893. In September of the same year Mr. McDivitt and A. R. Goddard formed a partnership firm to manufacture and sell the stretcher in the United States. They had but little capital to invest at that time, and this made it up-hill work in getting it started. In April, 1894, Mr. McDivitt sold his half interest to George M. Allen, of Beloit, Wis., and C. C. Atwood, of Albion, Wis. In November, 1895, Mr. Atwood accepted an offer to sell his interest from E. W. Goddard, of Terryville,

A. R. GODDARD OPERATING STRETCHER AND TACKER.

THE STRETCHER AND TACKER.

Conn., and the firm name was changed to The Goddard & Allen Co. The business was started at the beginning of the panic, which made it all the harder for the new venture. Notwithstanding, the firm had a good year in 1895, and there has been a decided increase in the business so far this year. Their goods are handled exclusively through agents, as Mr. Goddard believes this is the only way to sell and introduce a new household article. If every family in the United States had a Belvidere Carpet Stretcher, the white-winged dove of peace would rule the day during the house-cleaning and moving time period. Those who have tested this remarkable machine unhesitatingly pronounce it the most practical Carpet Stretcher and Tacker ever offered to the public. The writer has seen all kinds of Carpet Stretchers, and can conscientiously say that "The Belvidere" excels anything ever seen.

This Stretcher is made of the very best material, with an eye to durability, good service, and neatness; the handle and stretcher-bar being made of hard maple, the driving-rod of Bessemer steel, with case-hardened tip. A lever draws the carpet to its place, an automatic device places a tack in position, and a single blow of the driving-rod sets it firmly in the floor. The operator maintains an upright position; his weight on the carpet and Stretcher assists instead of retards its working. The leverage is so great that it requires little effort to bring the carpet to the desired tension on the floor, and it is held firmly in position by weight of operator until tacked down.

O. H. WRIGHT, SR.

Belvidere boasts of her brilliant sons and influential men, whose fame spreads throughout the entire state of Illinois. And well she may for there is no city of the size in the state that has furnished so many able men. Chief among those whose names give credit to the city is the Hon. O. H. Wright, Sr. His past is one of which any man might well feel proud—a record of signal successes in the business world and professional world, a succession of honors in public life.

He is one of the city's oldest residents, coming here in 1855. He was born in Green county, N. Y., in 1827. Early in life Mr. Wright became a school teacher. Before coming west he was principal of Greenville (N. Y.) Academy. His first experience in Belvidere was teaching. He organized and became principal of the Union school. Later he turned to the study of law and read with General Stephen Hurlbut, being admitted to the bar in 1864. In those early days Belvidere

HON. O. H. WRIGHT.

had a corps of able attorneys and Mr. Wright was obliged to work hard to establish a law practice. He was called the "teacher lawyer" by his opponents, but they soon found the "teacher lawyer" was made of the right kind of stuff. He soon demonstrated his ability and his name as an eloquent practitioner became known in all the adjoining counties. When the Republican party was in its incipiency, Mr. Wright was an advocate of its principles. The first political speech he ever made was in 1856 for John C. Fremont who was defeated for the presidency by Buchanan. He was one of the organizers of the party and is now an enthusiastic Republican. He says he always expects to be one.

Shortly after he was admitted to the bar he was elected city magistrate and at various periods he has held the offices of city clerk, master of chancery, and was county assessor under the revenue law eight years. In 1878 the people sent Mr.

Wright to the state legislature and kept him there for three successive terms. Subsequently Governor Oglesby appointed him one of the three penitentiary commissioners, which by the way, is not only a responsible position but great honor attaches to it as well. In this capacity he served four years.

Mr. Wright started the first agricultural implement warehouse in Belvidere. He erected several business blocks. One of those on South State street was destroyed by fire in 1883, entailing a loss of $10,000 without any insurance, a serious loss for Mr. Wright.

Mr. Wright is spending the evening of his life with as much freedom from cares as his business will permit. While he is at the head of the firm of O. H. Wright & Co., his son Omar takes the weight of responsibility from his shoulders.

RESIDENCE OF OMAR H. WRIGHT, JR.
PHOTO BY CLARK & NOTT.

He has large financial interests in Belvidere which necessarily require attention. He is a stockholder and director of the People's bank, and is the owner of considerable real estate. Mr. Wright has a cottage at Geneva Lake, Wis., where he spends the summer, and also considerable property in Chicago. He has done more than his part in the upbuilding of the city and well deserves a rest. Mr. Wright is loved and respected by all who know him.

O. H. WRIGHT AND CO.

The firm of O. H. Wright & Son, dealers in lumber and coal, commenced operations at its present location on Pleasant street, April 1, 1889. From the beginning success attended the enterprise, and the stock and facilities were increased, until now the heaviest and most varied demands are promptly met. June 1, 1893, John G. Tripp was admitted as a partner, the firm name changed to that of O. H. Wright & Co., and the buying of grain added to the business. Mr. Tripp's long experience in the grain market well qualifies him for the management of this department. The offices and yards are located on both sides of the railroad track, one block west of State street, and cover an extended space of ground. Purchases of lumber are made in large lots at the mills in Wisconsin and Michigan, of coal at the mines, and other material at first hand. Nearly everything in the way of building supplies is handled, with the addition of drain tile in all sizes. Hon. O. H. Wright, Sr. retains a supervisory interest in the business, but the active management devolves on the other partners, Omar H. Wright, Jr. and Mr. Tripp. The high position attained by this firm is notable even in this city of commercial surprises.

OMAR H. WRIGHT, JR.

A partner in the firm of O. H. Wright & Co., was born at Belvidere in 1867, and graduated from the high school in 1884. In 1885 he was tendered and accepted a position in the purchasing department of the Illinois state penitentiary at Joliet, and remained there three years. Entering the lumber and coal business in 1889, his energy and talent contributed to the early placing of the enterprise in the van of successful business houses. He was elected alderman from the first ward in April, 1891, and re-elected in 1893, serving four years. He was among the organizers of the Belvidere Telephone Company, and is now its secretary. His marriage to Miss Sarah Burton took place at Batavia, Illinois, February 10, 1892. They have one son. In the fall of 1894 he completed one of the largest and handsomest residences in the city. It is situated at the corner of State and Sixth streets, in Highland addition, and was erected under plans from Frank P. Allen, a leading architect of Grand Rapids, Mich., at an expense of $6,000. It was fitted with every convenience and elegantly furnished. Last November it was partially destroyed by fire, but immediately rebuilt. Mr. Wright is a representative of the younger and progressive type of merchants whose value in a growing city is highly estimated.

H. H. RUBIN.
PHOTO BY YOUNDT.

H. H. RUBIN.

"Rubin's Bakery" has for many years been a household phrase in Belvidere. At one time almost the only establishment of the kind in the city, it has been enlarged, in keeping with the general progress, until everything in the line required by home-providers is now promptly supplied. It follows in this undertaking, as with most others, that a faithful adherence to the one special line ensures proficiency and the best resultant service. This was the policy adopted by Mr. Rubin years ago, and now followed. Mr. Rubin was born in Watertown, Wis.,

February 17, 1861. Receiving his education and learning his trade at Janesville, Wis., he came to Belvidere in 1880, and obtained employment with W. F. Zeigler, who was at that time the leading baker of the town. In 1883 occurred his marriage to Miss Rosa Fenwick. In 1887 he purchased Joseph Fenwick's bakery, and now carries on business at the same location. An idea of the extent to which provision is made for the public may be gained from the statement that he uses about 2,000 sacks of flour, 100 barrels of sugar, and 50 tierces of lard annually. Mr. Rubin is Treasurer of Kishwaukee Chapter, No. 90, R. A. M., and Past Grand of the local lodge of I. O. O. F. In 1894 the family residence at State

H. H. RUBIN'S RESIDENCE.

and Jackson streets was completed, and it is noted for being one of the handsomest and most commodious of the fine structures gracing that section of the city.

L. C. WILLARD.

The mercantile interests of any city would be incomplete without a first-class furniture establishment, such as is conducted by the gentleman whose name forms the subject of this article, and who may justly be regarded as one of Belvidere's safe, reliable and conservative business men. Mr. Willard is a practical and experienced furniture dealer, having been engaged in the business in Belvidere for quite a number of years; he knows when, how and where to buy furniture, at such prices that enable him to give his patrons the advantage, when purchasing of him, of the lowest possible prices of any similar establishment in the north-west. Mr. Willard is one of our active, energetic and enterprising business men, who keeps abreast of the times by always handling just what the public requires, as is so plainly evident by a casual glance at his well, immense and judiciously selected stock of furniture that is not excelled or equalled in variety, quality and prices in this section of the state, a fact that is being recognized and appreciated by not only his legion of patrons, but the public generally, and upon this hypothesis may properly be assigned the fundamental principle of his chief success and the immense and profitable trade, which reflects credit upon his good discretion, that he so successfully succeeded in establishing in Belvidere. His stock of parlor and bedroom sets, the most modern and latest style, together with tables, chairs, sofas, desks, rockers, and in fact everything to be found in a first-class establishment of a like character, is not only full and complete, but embraces such a choice selec-

RESIDENCE OF L. C. WILLARD.
PHOTO BY CLARK & NOTT.

tion as will be difficult to be seen elsewhere. In connection with this well regulated establishment is a first-class undertaking department, under the personal attention of Mr. Willard, who in this respect knows well the requirements of an undertaker, having served the people of Belvidere for the past twelve years, always giving perfect satisfaction.

JOHN C. FOOTE.

For a quarter of a century John C. Foote has conducted a drug store on South State street, and it is one of the leading establishments of the city. He was born in Hamilton, N. Y., September 20, 1841, and received a thorough preparatory education in early youth. He graduated at Colgate university in 1864, and succeeded his father, Hon. John J. Foote, in the drug business at Hamilton in 1865.

His marriage to Miss Helen, daughter of Judge Samuel B. Garvin, of New York city, took place in 1867. Coming to Belvidere in 1869, he founded his present business in 1870. His children are: Mary Helen, May Garvin, Florence Annette and John Garvin.

Mr. Foote has always been an ardent Republican, and while never caring to hold office, has yet constantly and with effect interested himself in political affairs. Few have shown a livelier appreciation of the needs of the city or greater willingness to aid in forwarding every measure calculated to develop its resources. Prominent in business circles, church affairs and socially, Mr. Foote is highly esteemed, and has the confidence and regard of the public.

RESIDENCE OF JOHN C. FOOTE.

SABIN BROS., DRY GOODS.

The metropolitan dry goods store now conducted by Sabin Bros. was established in February, 1866, by their father, David D. Sabin, the firm being D. D. Sabin & Co. Subsequently H. B. Sykes took the place of the retiring partner, P. R. Sabin, and continued in the firm until 1884, when D. D. Sabin became sole proprietor. Being capable and experienced in the dry goods line, Mr. Sabin commanded a prosperous patronage. He showed his enterprise when, in 1876, he erected the large business block now occupied by Sabin Bros. Mr. Sabin conducted the business until 1889, when his son Sidney A. was admitted to partnership. In 1894 the firm Sabin & Son was succeeded by Eugene F. and Sidney A. as Sabin Bros. Prior to this change Eugene F. Sabin had been identified for fifteen years with the large wholesale house of John V. Farwell & Co., and this wide experience gave him peculiar and fitting qualifications which gave added vigor to the business. Sidney A. Sabin, it may be said, "grew up in the business." After completing his school work he became associated with the business, and spent twelve years in the dry goods trade. The Sabin brothers make a team that is hard to equal. Their motto is "Best qualities always," and the term "The ever busy store" has been applied to their dry goods house. Their stock is always up-to-date, well selected and complete in all departments, and only in the larger cities can its equal be found.

FRANK W. PLANE.

Very prominent among the older manufacturing establishments of this city, and indeed of the country, is the Plane Screen Door Manufactory. It was started by Mr. Plane in 1880. The entire product for that year was 3,500 doors. The increase in the output has been gradual but large, until now 150,000 doors are annually shipped, requiring 200 cars. The factory is located on Pleasant street and solidly built of stone. The average force employed

D. D. SABIN.
PHOTO BY CLARK & NOTT.

is twenty-five, at the head of which is Millard Boyce, whose engagement began with the business. Window screens, wire cloth and hardware specialties are also made and carried. Mr. Plane is the local manager of the Central Union Telephone Exchange. In the spring of 1895 the entire city line was reconstructed at an expense of $20,000. The service is at all times prompt and reliable. Mr. Frank W. Plane was born in Belvidere, November 15, 1846. He is a son of John Plane, one of the oldest residents. At the age of twenty he entered his father's hardware store as clerk. His marriage to Miss E. L. Post took place in May, 1875. They have one child, a lad of eleven years. Himself and wife are connected

F. W. PLANE.
PHOTO BY CLARK & NOTT.

with the South Baptist Church, and as one of the trustees he has rendered long and valuable service, while Mrs. Plane is the efficient treasurer of the society. Mr. Plane is an active, public-spirited citizen, heartily coöperating with his business associates in promoting the interests of his native city.

R. C. FRITZ.

One of the enterprises exceedingly valuable to a building community is that of brick-making. It ensures an always available supply of an indispensable article. Such an industry is that of R. C. Fritz, located in almost the heart of the city. It was known at an early day that a bed of clay, considerable in extent and of excellent quality, underlaid the site of the present kilns. Efforts to utilize this deposit were made at intervals, but complete success had never resulted until the

SCENE AT THE BRICK YARD OF R. C. FRITZ.

present energetic proprietor began the essay. At the time of his arrival from Gridley, Ill, nine years ago, the product could hardly be given away. Mr. Fritz had faith, however, that first-class brick could be turned out. New machinery was purchased, and numerous experiments were made, but there were discouragements and costly failures. In 1892 the plant was entirely wiped out by flood. Then fire destroyed the sheds and a large part of the machinery. Yet the plucky young proprietor was not dismayed, but rebuilt and enlarged, and finally placed the enterprise on a firm footing. He now employs in the busy season about twenty-five men, and turns out 2,000,000 bricks a year. The National Company was supplied with 100,000 for the outside finishing of the great building erected last summer, while its contract for the inferior inside walls was let to foreign firms. This is a high testimonial from a competent source. The reputation of the product is now established, and contractors from a distance are sending orders in liberal volume. Belvidere brick have no superior in the state. Mr. Fritz is an active member of the Methodist church and superintendent of its Sabbath school. He also holds other offices. An energetic, capable, reliable business man, and worthy citizen, his success in the face of many obstacles is a source of gratification to the community.

THE HOTEL EVANS.

This well-known hostelry was purchased and re-named by Mr. Fred J. Evans in 1894. Its location on State street, size, arrangement and furnishing combine to make it inferior to none other in the city. Immediately after obtaining control it was entirely refitted by the present proprietor with all the modern belongings of a first-class hotel, at large expense. It has steam heat, electric lights and annunciators, barber shop, baths, spacious sample-rooms, free train service, and bills of

THE HOTEL EVANS.
PHOTO BY CLARK & NOTT.

table-fare that attract liberal patronage from city residents as well as travelers. As Mr. Evans personally manages the hotel, its guests are always assured of the most perfect care and attention, which fact, together with a moderate tariff of charges, invariably ensures a revisit from those who have once accepted its hospitalities. Mr. Henry Sweet, long a resident of Belvidere, is in charge of the office, a position held for some years, and ably seconds the proprietor in rendering acceptable service to the public.

CAPT. JAMES M. HUMPHREY.

In keeping with the general advancement that has made the Belvidere of to-day are the progressive ideas of the dealers in furniture. Where a few years ago limited quarters and moderate displays were sufficient, now extensive warehouses and great variety are considered indispensable. Probably the new building erected by Captain Humphrey on South State street, and occupied nearly in its entirety as salesrooms, is unsurpassed by any similar structure in this part of the state. It is 44x90 feet in extent, two stories and basement in height, of brick and stone, with a highly ornate front, and is one of the handsomest business blocks in the city. It is filled with a stock from which may be equipped the plainest or most pretentious dwelling. The undertaking department carries a full line of funeral furnishings, and the details of embalming and burial are attended to in accordance with approved methods. Captain Humphrey was born August 31, 1840, at Danville, Ohio. His parents, Thomas J. and Caroline A. Humphrey, came to Boone county in 1840, and located on a farm ten miles south of Belvidere.

HUMPHREY BLOCK AND J. M. HUMPHREY'S FURNITURE STORE.

They emigrated from Rhode Island at an early date, and first went to Ohio, settling on a tract of land given his grandfather for services performed in the Revolutionary war, which was perforce accepted in lieu of cash. Captain Humphrey was educated at Beloit College, and took a commercial course in Chicago. He was married to Miss Rosirah Newton in Flora, this county, December 25, 1862. They have five children, one son and four daughters, all of whom are married. In 1864 he raised and commanded a company enlisted for the United States service, and which became Company C, One Hundred and Forty-second Infantry. For its share in the defense of St. Louis it received the thanks of President Lincoln, through his Secretary of War Stanton. Returning to Belvidere Captain Humphrey engaged as a commercial traveler, farmer and hardware merchant, in the order mentioned, opening a furniture store about five years ago. One of his brothers attained the rank of brigadier general, and another captain of cavalry, during the war. He is a member of Hurlbut Post, G. A. R., and of the M. W. A. Enterprising and public-spirited, Captain Humphrey keeps in line with the makers of modern Belvidere.

WM. SEWELL.

In his own building, which by the way, is one of the best in town, Mr. Sewell conducts a carriage business on an extensive scale. His repository on North State street is a credit to Belvidere. Mr. Sewell was born in Caledonia, this county. His father was Isaac Sewell, one of the county's sturdy pioneers. Mr. Sewell learned the carriage making trade in Beloit, Wis., where he had considerable experience in this line. Prior to moving to Beloit he held the office of township assessor for Caledonia for several years. Coming to Belvidere about twenty

WM. SEWELL'S BLOCK AND G. A. R. HALL.
PHOTO BY CLARK & NOTT.

years ago, he was for six years the expert and right-hand man for Captain Heywood, one of the leading machinery dealers. He was full of vigor and enterprise and launched into business for himself. Few business men have been more successful. An evidence of this fact is the sightly building erected by himself, in 1892, on the second floor of which is the Grand Army hall and which with the necessary adjuncts cover a large space. Mr. Sewell deals in fine carriages, wagons, sleighs, harness, etc., and does a large annual business.

The North Belvidere school board, on which he is serving his second term, conferred an honor on him, and placed a great responsibility in his hands during the past summer. The magnificent new $25,000 school edifice, a cut of which appears elsewhere, was constructed under his superintendency, he being at that time chairman of the building committee. Mr. Sewell is held in high esteem as a citizen.

RESIDENCE OF F. S. ROWAN.
PHOTO BY CLARK & NOTT.

PROPERTY OF F. S. ROWAN.
PHOTO BY CLARK & NOTT.

F. S. ROWAN.

"Just say I'm in the real estate business," said F. S. Rowan, when a representative of "Belvidere Illustrated" approached him. Mr. Rowan is modest, and dislikes too great a prominence. His magnificent residence shown herewith is a pride of the city. Mr. Rowan is president of the Gas Company, and a member of the South Belvidere school board. He is a man of high standing in financial circles, and is contributing his full share to the advancement of Belvidere. His real estate business is extensive.

THE WHITMAN-STARR BLOCK.

JOHN C. STARR.

John C. Starr has been in business in Belvidere for thirty-five consecutive years. He bears the proud distinction of being the second oldest business man in this city in point of continuous business activity. He was born in Whitehall, N. Y., in 1839, and lived there until his parents followed the western exodus in 1855. On October 13th of that year the family located in Belvidere. H. G. Starr, the father, was an expert harness maker and his son, John C., followed in his footsteps and became associated with him in business. After spending a year in Belvidere the Starrs moved to Forreston, Ogle county and then the head of the family embarked in the harness business. In 1860 John C. Starr who had always longed to get back to Belvidere, took up his residence in this city again and from that day he has not had the least thought of locating elsewhere. Mr. Starr is at present located in one of the new, modern and substantial business blocks on South State street which he erected himself last summer. He carries one of the largest and most complete lines of harness in northern Illinois.

Mr. Starr has held several honorary offices in this city and has had much experience in local public affairs. He is a careful and conservative gentleman and is one of Belvidere's staunchest business men.

WATKINS AND BURNS.

Less than two years ago the gentlemen composing this firm opened a comparatively small stock of dry goods in one of the Rider buildings on South State street, and their record has been one of uninterrupted advancement. At the present time, occupying one of the most perfectly appointed store-rooms in Northern Illinois, their sales are not exceeded by those of any other similar establishment in the city. The new location is in Central block, which was completed August 1, 1895, and upon which date the firm took possession of quarters especially fitted for its use. The floor space is 22x125; the fixtures are of recent design and include every convenience; bundle and cash carriers are used, and the store is warmed and lighted by furnaces and gas. Ten clerks care for their immense trade. The stock carried is, for extent and quality, far beyond the average in a

E. J. WATKINS.
PHOTO BY CLARK & NOTT.

T. F. BURNS.
PHOTO BY CLARK & NOTT.

city of this size. It is kept completely assorted by the modern method of frequent purchase. Under the three headings: Dry goods, carpets and cloaks, are included many subdivisions, all representing the most desirable products of the loom and workshop. The enterprising proprietors have achieved a success that is phenomenal, even in this day of rapid progression.

The senior partner of the above firm was born in the town of Flora, this county, December 17, 1860. His parents, J. B. and Ann Watkins, came to this part of the country, the former in 1842 and the latter in 1839. On their marriage they settled on a farm in Flora, where they resided for many years. Mr. E. J. Watkins, after completing his education, turned his attention to the dry goods business, beginning as a clerk in 1880, and retaining this position thirteen years.

RESIDENCE OF W. D. CORNWELL.

He was married in 1883 to Miss Ida E. Woolverton, of Belvidere. They have two daughters, one of eleven and the other of nine years. Mr. Watkins is a member of the American Legion of Honor.

T. F. Burns, the junior member, born at Belvidere, January 29, 1867. His parents, C. F. and Mary Burns, came to Belvidere in 1865. He was educated at the public schools, and after a varied preparatory experience, settled down to the dry goods business, which he has followed for many years. His marriage to Miss Elizabeth Quinn, of Elgin, took place April 30, 1890. They have three children, the eldest a son of three years. He is the treasurer of the Home Forum, a member of the M. W. A., and one of Belvidere's most progressive and successful merchants.

CORNWELL & CHAPPEL.

The members of this leading real estate firm began operations in February, 1895, and have since then prosecuted a most successful business. Their familiarity with both city and country property and skillful negotiation of deals, together with perfect reliability, have attracted a large clientage, and resulted in mutual satisfaction and profit. Some of the largest transactions of the year have been consummated through their agency. They not only attend to the transfer of property, but negotiate loans, rent houses and stores, and perform every service related to the business. Their success is in perfect keeping with the progress of the city, to which they have in no small degree contributed.

WILLIAM D. CORNWELL.

was born at Brantford, Canada, March 27, 1833. He came to Illinois with his parents in 1845. His father settled on a track of land in Caledonia township, and the son remained on the home-farm until arriving at the age of fifteen. He was

REV. J. G. ROCKENBACH.
PHOTO BY CLARK & NOTT.

then apprenticed to the mason's trade for three years. In 1857 he located on the farm he still owns, in the township mentioned. He worked at his trade until 1867, when he went to California and engaged in the lumber business. In 1871 Mr. Cornwell followed his trade in Pueblo and Denver, Col. On returning to this county he resumed residence on the farm, and prosecuted his trade until 1890, when he was elected county treasurer, and then moved to Belvidere. His marriage to Miss Catherine Chappel took place in 1857. His present wife was Miss Mary A. Getten. Both Mr. Cornwell and his wife are prominent members of the Methodist Episcopal church, and the former has rendered conspicuous service to the denomination as a lay preacher.

W. H. CHAPPEL.

Mr. Chappel, associated with Mr. Cornwell in business, was born in Stafford, New York state, April 16, 1842. He came to Boone county in 1855. Learning the carpenter's trade, he followed it until the earlier period of the war, when he enlisted in Company "K," 95th Illinois, August 13, 1862. Performing the full three years' service, he was honorably mustered out. He was married to Miss Rosaltha M. Corning in 1867. They have two daughters, one of whom is married. Their residence in Belvidere dates from the fall of '95. Mr. Chappel's business engagements have required his absence from the county for many years, but his arrangements are now such as to make a permanent residence possible.

WILLIAM H. PIEL.

W. H. Piel, who is styled "The Logan Avenue Grocer," is an example of how a pushing, energetic young man finds his way to the front. Six years ago he

W. H. PIEL.

started in business with F. J. Evans, and for the past four years has been in trade alone. His grocery house is one of the most popular in town. It is located in a handsome new building with fine plate glass front, and these elegant quarters give Mr. Piel an advantage over some of his competitors. He carries a complete stock of goods and is doing a successful business.

Having been born and reared in Belvidere, Mr. Piel is well acquainted. He has a reputation for honest dealing and fair treatment that is consistently maintained.

OSGOOD & ANDREWS.

Everybody in Belvidere knows genial Major R. E. Osgood. Years ago he established a livery business here.

When the fierce struggle of the 60's began he enlisted in the 6th Ohio Cavalry and distinguished himself in service. First a private, then second lieutenant, later

OSGOOD & ANDREWS' LIVERY.
PHOTO BY CLARK & NOTT.

first lieutenant, next captain and finally major, his war record is a brilliant one and needs no eulogy.

After the war he came to Belvidere and bought out Woodard & Lease's livery. Since that time, thirty years ago, the major has stood by his post. A year ago Elliott Andrews, son of Deacon Andrews, who has made his home with Major Osgood for some years, was taken into partnership. Mr. Andrews is one of the hustling young men of the city and a fresh impetus was given to the business. Despite the bicycle, the major says the past year was one of the best he has ever had. He gives Mr. Andrews much credit for this. The livery business is conducted in good quarters on Whitney street. The large barn was built by Major Osgood in 1871, after fire had burned him out. Osgood & Andrews are one of Belvidere's best firms and are deserving of their prosperity.

COMMERCE BLOCK.
OWNED BY J. S. EDELSTEIN.

JACOB S. EDELSTEIN.

J. S. EDELSTEIN.

One of the most notable instances in this community of the rapid rise to position and a competency from humble beginnings is that of Jacob S. Edelstein. Born in Courland, on the coast of the Baltic sea, in 1857, he cut loose from the fatherland in 1881, and sailed for the United States. Landing almost penniless, he maintained himself by strenuous effort until 1883, when he came to Belvidere and started in business in the smallest possible way. Everybody here remembers the little store on State street, crowded with inexpensive dry goods, and the always present and industrious proprietor. In 1884 he was married to Miss Johanna Barry. His assiduousness was redoubled, and in 1885 a larger store-room was required, that selected being in the Ames block. In 1890 he built the Edelstein block, a handsome double-store structure, into one of which he moved. Here for six years he conducted a flourishing business, and became one of the leading merchants of the city. Outside operations added to his means, and the Buchanan block was purchased as an investment. This building has recently been remodeled and is a handsome ornament to the principal thoroughfare. The elegant residence now the property of Dr. Markley was built and occupied by Mr. Edelstein.— Mr. E.'s fine home is in the same neighborhood, where with his wife and three bright

THE EDELSTEIN BLOCK.

children he intends taking life with more ease for a time, having retired from business early in the present year. Mr. Edelstein's parents are still living in the old country, and it is his pleasurable duty to minister to their wants. His five brothers are each indebted to him for their start in business. Mr. Edelstein's career is but another illustration of the advancement that is possible in this country of boundless opportunity, and no other in like degree.

C. N. SMITH.

C. N. Smith, the genial postmaster, has made an enviable record in Belvidere. He was born in Bushnell, Ill., in 1862. In 1881 he came to this city and shortly

C. N. SMITH,
POSTMASTER.
PHOTO BY YOUNDT.

afterward began the manufacture of cigars. Ever since he located here he has taken an active hand in politics and his good work for the democracy gave him the postoffice. Mr. Smith has made an excellent official and has accomplished more for the public than any of his predecessors. First the office was entirely remodeled and refitted, but the most important improvement in the mail service was the establishment of the free delivery system which was brought about directly through the efforts of the postmaster.

Mr. Smith is closely allied with the democratic leaders of the state and is generally on "the inside." He is a clever, affable gentleman and has many friends.

HON. DU FAY A. FULLER,

Republican nominee for representative in the general assembly, was born in the town of Flora, in Boone county, about forty-four years ago. He has always resided on the farm where he was born, although as district manager of the Mutual Life Insurance Company of New York, he has an office in Belvidere. He is a son of Seymour and Eliza A. Fuller, who were among the early settlers of this county. What education he acquired was in the district school, and his early life was passed in such toil as is incident to a farmer's life. Mr. Fuller was the youngest son of the family, and the others, going early out into the world for themselves, seemed to render it necessary that Du Fay should remain at home. He has three brothers, James A., of Chicago, George H., a banker of Rockwell, Iowa, Charles E., of this city, and one sister, Mrs. F. S. Stockwell, of Cherry Valley. Mr. Fuller has been somewhat prominent in town matters in the town of Flora, and

HON. D. A. FULLER,
MEMBER OF THE ILLINOIS HOUSE OF REPRESENTATIVES.

has for several terms held the offices of justice of the peace and of township treasurer. He is a man of sturdy common sense, of unblemished character and of considerable business ability. That he fully possesses the confidence and esteem of those who know him best is evidenced from the fact that when he became a candidate for representative, at the primary election in his own town there was not a vote against him, and he had the enthusiastic support of all his neighbors. He is a member of the South Baptist church of Belvidere, of which both his parents were also members, and is also a Mason, an Odd Fellow and a member of several other fraternal societies. In 1875 he was married to Miss Jennie Robinson, of Cherry Valley, who died in 1895. One child preceded Mrs. Fuller to the other shore.

Mr. Fuller is socially a gentleman, an honest and honorable man, whom it is a pleasure to know.

LUKE WHEELER.

THE "STANDARD."

The *Standard* was established in 1851 by Ralph Roberts, its present propietor. It was not quite the first paper printed in Boone county, as about 1848-50 a venture had been made by a Mr. Snow, which was entitled the Belvidere *Republican*. Its existence was brief. The *Standard* was at first Democratic in politics, and continued in that faith until the breaking up of parties on the free-soil question, when the Whigs and free soil Democrats united and formed the present Republican party. It has since advocated Republican principles. Mr. Roberts and Elder L. W. Lawrence were delegates from Boone county to the first Republican convention at Bloomington, and listened to Abraham Lincoln's great speech on that occasion. When the *Standard* was established the railroad was completed to Huntley only, and the handpress and boxes of type were hauled by team from that place over muddy roads at large expense. At that time the south side of the river could boast of but two small frame buildings. From 1851 to 1860 the *Standard* was the only paper published in this county. The *Standard* first occupied a part of the building now known as Wing's flats, on East Madison street, but was removed in the same year to a wooden structure on Lincoln avenue, just east of State street. In 1854 the brick block on the corner, in which was then the post-office, was destroyed by fire, which also partly burned the

RALPH ROBERTS.
PHOTO BY YOUNDT.

building tenanted by the *Standard* office. The printing outfit was then moved to a building opposite the American House, but shortly after transferred to the brick building now occupied by the *Standard*. The *Standard* is now in its forty-fifth volume. Its veteran editor has been at the helm through all these years, and has witnessed the growth of Belvidere from a village of four hundred inhabitants to its present size. Mr. Roberts was born in East Hartford, Conn., in 1822, and, after serving his apprenticeship in New York City, came to Chicago in 1843. He first located in Woodstock, and published there the Woodstock *Democrat*, and from thence removed to Belvidere.

A. H. KEELER.

ALSON H. KEELER.

Alson H. Keeler, senior member of Keeler & Truitt, publishers of the *Belvidere Northwestern*, was born in this county in 1854; has resided here almost continuously, and therefore needs no introduction to the people of Belvidere and Boone county. He acquired his early education in the country schools, afterwards being a student in the North Belvidere schools, and at Beloit College. His parents, Mr. and Mrs. Warren Keeler, were early settlers in this township. He has been connected with newspapaper work and the printing business since 1875, in the various capacities from "devil" to editor. In the spring of 1888 he assumed sole proprietorship of the *Northwestern*, and did not part with any of this valuable property until last fall (1895), when Mr. Charles R. Truitt secured a half interest in the business. Mr. Keeler still owns the fine building in which the *Northwestern* is published, and which he erected in 1892 especially for the business.

Incidentally it may be remarked that the *Northwestern* ranks high among the leading country journals of the state.

Mr. Keeler was married in 1880 to Miss Edith A. Swasey, daughter of the late Hon. Samuel Swasey. They have one son, Laurence S., born December 23, 1882.

CHARLES R. TRUITT.

Charles R. Truitt, one of the editors and proprietors of the *Northwestern*, was born on a farm in Montgomery county, Illinois, in 1858. He was educated in the public schools, at the Hillsboro Academy, and graduated at Williston Seminary, Easthampton, Mass., and at Lafayette College, Easton, Pa. While at Williston Seminary he took the second prize for excellence in oratory. After leaving school, he taught for a few years, being assistant principal of the Hillsboro High School for two years. Having a liking for journalism, he purchased the

C. R. TRUITT.

Hillsboro *Journal* in 1881, and after publishing it successfully for thirteen years, sold it. He held the office of township treasurer for ten years, and during that time handled over $100,000. He was also a director in and president of the Hillsboro Building and Improvement Association. In 1889 he was appointed United States Deputy Collector of Internal Revenue for the Eighth Illinois District. Mr. Truitt has always been an ardent Republican and has represented his party at state, congressional and county conventions. He is a member of the Odd Fellows and Modern Woodmen. He is married and has a family of three children. He is a member of the Illinois Press Association, and was for a number of years correspondent for such metropolitan papers as the St. Louis *Globe-Democrat*, Chicago *Tribune*, *Inter Ocean* and *Record*.

In October, 1895, he purchased a full one-half interest in the Belvidere *Northwestern*, one of the most prominent and influential Republican journals in northern Illinois, and now considers himself fully identified with the interests of Boone county.

N. M. YOUNDT.

N. M. YOUNDT.

The oldest photographic establishment in Belvidere is that of N. M. Youndt. It has survived the careers, brief or extended, of nineteen other similar enterprises. Its proprietor's adherence to a line once marked out exemplifies the truth that persistence and faith invariably lead to success. This extended business life is also a tribute to the artistic excellence of his work. Mr. Youndt was born in Trenton, Ohio, May 10, 1847, but acquired the details of the art during a sojourn of several years in Philadelphia, where his studies were prosecuted under McKlees, a noted German art photographer and chemist. He came to Belvidere in 1879 from Batavia. His experience in picture-making covers a period of thirty years, and includes the production of every known style and method after that of Daguerre. This constant application has resulted in a perfect familiarity with all approved processes; and the adoption of the newest ideas of value as developed by the specialists of the profession is a practice regularly followed. His studio on State street contains many illustrations of the finest effects produced by late

AT THE BEND OF THE KISHWAUKEE RIVER.
PHOTO BY W H ROBINSON.

V. I. CLARK.

methods Mr. Youndt's specialty is that of portraits, a number of those recently taken appearing on these pages, but he also accepts commissions for outside and interior work on residences. A careful, painstaking, thoroughly well-posted artist, with taste and judgment, Mr. Youndt may be well assured of public appreciation. His marriage to Miss Lydia M. Longcor, youngest daughter of the late Samuel Longcor, took place in Belvidere January 1, 1880. A couple of years ago the fine residence on Hurlbut avenue was completed, and is an acquisition to that street of beautiful homes. He is fraternally connected with the Masons, Odd Fellows, Knights of the Maccabees and United Workmen.

CLARK AND NOTT.

The members of this representative firm have been extensively engaged in the photographic business for the past four years. They have two galleries—one in this city and one at Marengo. That in Marengo is managed by Mr. Nott, and was opened two years ago. The gallery in Belvidere has been in operation since 1893, and is supervised by Mr. Clark. Their experience has been one of uniform success, which is very largely due to the quality of the work produced and the artistic taste exhibited. Every detail of picture-making from the taking of the negative to the finished transfer is the result of facilities pertaining to their establishments. Outside aid is never invoked. Only the best ma-

J. P. NOTT.

terials are used, the paper being of the first quality and given the new "Platinette" finish, so popular now. The gloss surface makes the pictures waterproof, and is the only process ensuring durability. Many of the superb illustrations and portraits in this volume are evidence of their skill and thorough methods. A branch of the art to which great attention is paid is that of water-color portraits. The examples of this treatment on display are exquisitely beautiful. The flash-light is used with great frequency for interior views, while landscape and exterior work is made a specialty. The firm also deals largely in

RESIDENCE OF F. B. ROWAN.
PHOTO BY CLARK & NOTT.

cameras, amateur's supplies and frames. Provided with all needful accessories, and devoting their entire time to the study and developing of the art, the utmost satisfaction necessarily follows every order.

DR. F. B. ROWAN, D. V. S. AND V. D.

Dr. Rowan is an honorary graduate of the Chicago Veterinary College, and has practiced his profession in this city for about seven years. Conveniently located at 15 Logan avenue, his services are in constant demand by those who appreciate humane methods and skillful treatment when applied to man's noblest servant. Not long ago he completed one of the finest residences in the city, occupying a choice site on Logan avenue, a reproduction of which structure accompanies this sketch. Averse to conspicuous mention, Dr. Rowan is nevertheless one of our most valued and esteemed citizens.

W. H. CORNELL.

Without builders no building could be done. One of the most successful contractors and builders of whom Belvidere can boast is W. H. Cornell. Mr. Cornell thinks highly of Belvidere, for it has been his home all his life. He was born three miles south of this city in 1853. His father, L. P. Cornell, came here from New York in 1843, when this town was as scattered as a boy's first moustache. When W. H. was four years old his parents moved to town. He began early in life to learn the carpenter's trade. Sixteen years ago he started out as a contractor, subsequently forming a partnership with W. M. Marean. All over the city are magnificent structures, monuments to their skill and ability. To mention all the buildings which Mr. Cornell constructed under contract would require too much space. Chief among them, however, are the South Belvidere brick school No. 1, W. D. Swail's fine home, and Dr. F. S. Whitman's beautiful residence. For the past few years Mr. Cornell has been in business by himself, and the amount of large jobs awarded him is evidence of his standing as a builder. The past summer's work included H. H. Rubin's costly home, the Witbeck-Kellogg double business block, M. E. Bowley's improvement, Henry Heywood's $5,000 residence, and a score of cottages ranging in cost from $1,000 to $1,500. Mr. Cornell is successful at his business, and all for whom he has done work praise his skill. He is a stockholder of the Belvidere Electric Light Company. No one in the city is more enthusiastic over the city's prospects than he.

JAMES WALSH,

manufacturer of bottled goods, is represented in Belvidere by John Dooley, who has been local manager ever since the office was first opened in 1893. He transacts a wholesale and retail business, making the family bottle trade a specialty. Barreled beer is also handled, and more than half the trade of Belvidere in this product is now supplied by this establishment. The beverages furnished by this concern fill an extended list. Among them are: Ginger ale, mead, mineral water, bottled beer, ale, porter and cider. It is also agent for Miller's Milwaukee beer. Purity of ingredients, and first qualities always, together with reasonable prices and prompt service, are the factors which have enabled the proprietor to build up and maintain a very large and increasing business at this point.

J. H. WOODS.

Mr. Woods settled in Belvidere about five years ago, and formed a partnership in the livery business, which continued until last year, when he became entire owner. He was born in Washington county, Pennsylvania, May 19, 1847, and came West with his parents eight years later. His father and mother, William and Amelia C. Woods, located on a farm in Franklin, De Kalb county, in which section of the country the subject of this sketch resided until coming to this city. January 1, 1868, he married Miss Marilla Shannon, of Flora, this county. They have two children, Clarence H., nineteen, and Bertha A., twelve years of age. The commodious stables, illustrated above, and used by Mr. Woods, are at a central location on Logan avenue, and house an extensive outfit of reliable drivers and modern vehicles, which meets every demand that can reasonably be made. He also buys and sells horses, and has a large patronage in this branch of his business, because of superior judgement in choice. Boarding and care of transients are features given particular attention. Mr. Woods is not at all averse to having it understood that he is solidly Republican in politics, and that he has the strongest kind of faith in the future of a city holding out so many promises to the business man. He also takes a lively interest in educational matters, which fact was recognized in his selection as a member of the School Board, a position he now fills, and which the public exhibited wisdom in making. With his family he occupies a fine residence on Pearl street, in one of the most desirable quarters of the city.

J. H. WOODS' LIVERY STABLE.
PHOTO BY CLARK & NOTT.

A. F. WHEELER.

If indefatigable effort, almost unaided, progressive business methods and active interest in enterprises of a public nature make successful and valued citizens, then A. F. Wheeler must be accounted as being among the first. Coming to Belvidere in 1889, he immediately engaged in the clothing and boot and shoe business, which has since been continuously followed. The results of his application and the appreciation of the community are to be noted in the large establishment on South State street, of which he is sole proprietor. Here is displayed everything in the line of apparel for men and boys demanded by dressy and practical buyers. A specialty to which much attention is given is that of the "Happy Home" ready-to-wear suits, of which immense quantities have been sold. The store is large, the stock fills it and is kept well up to date, and the service is always reliable. Mr. Wheeler's father, George G., and mother, Helen M., came to Boone county in 1842 from New York state, settling on a farm in Flora. Their son, A. F., was born in the township just named, September 16, 1863. He was married to Miss Cora Belle Clarke, September 7, 1892, at Muskegon, Mich. Their children are Violet Lucile and Florence Emily, the oldest not quite three years of age. He is a member of the Masonic order, Royal Arcanum and Knights of Pythias. With pleasant home environment, an extended social acquaintance and a prosperous business, Mr. Wheeler occupies an enviable position among the leading and enterprising merchants of the city.

A. F. WHEELER.
PHOTO BY CLARK & NOTT.

THE BELVIDERE STEAM LAUNDRY.

This extensive plant, opposite the National Manufactory, has been successfully operated by the present proprietor for five years. The amount of business transacted, coming from every part of the city, increases with each year, and now requires the constant employment of a large force. The equipment is of the most modern description, several new machines having recently been added, and the greatest care is taken to turn out work which will equal that demanded in the large cities. All materials from the coarsest cotton to daintiest lace are accepted, and laundered in the finest style. The system is now so perfected that an order can be filled, in case of necessity, within two hours. The collection and delivery service is always prompt and reliable. Miss Alta Miller, the proprietor, has followed the business for over twenty-five years, fifteen of which were passed in Chicago. From that city she went to Rock Island, coming from the latter place to Belvidere. Familiarity with every detail, gathered in this extended experience, ensures the perfect finish of consignments from families and individuals, and the satisfaction of every patron.

GRAY & MORSE'S COAL YARDS.

GRAY & MORSE.

Three years ago last fall H. R. Gray and S. E. Morse formed a partnership in the grain and hay business. So marked was their success in that line they determined to branch out, and a few months ago added coal and feed to the goods carried. A feed warehouse 24 by 60 and coal sheds 18 by 80 were built, thus making it a valuable property and affording abundant facilities.

Mr. Gray is fifty-one years old and was a farmer living north of town for twenty-nine years. Mr. Morse was born north of the city forty years ago. He remained on his father's farm until a comparatively recent date. The firm has always enjoyed a good trade, and during the past year business has been especially brisk. Both are men of high standing. They are upright in their dealings and making new friends every day.

LEWIS H. STURGES.

Lewis H. Sturges has made an enviable reputation as an architect. His change of residence from Rockford to Belvidere occurred three years ago. A skillful architect is a valuable acquisition to a growing city, and it did not take Mr. Sturges long to demonstrate his ability in this line and build up a fine

LEWIS H. STURGES.

patronage. One of his first essays was the drawing of plans for the Murch and Pettit block, one of the handsomest business structures in the city. Other business buildings for which he furnished plans are the P. R. Kennedy block, the Ransom store, and J. S. Edelstein's fine new "Commerce" block. One of the prettiest residences in the city—the Capt. Hick's house on Pearl street—was planned and built by Mr. Sturges. Another fine house for which he drew plans is the H. F. Bowley residence on Whitney street. Besides the above mentioned structures he has furnished plans for scores of other buildings, and in every instance has given satisfaction. Mr. Sturges is also a contractor and builder. He began the following of this trade early in life, and there is no more expert carpenter and builder in Bel-

S. PEPPER S RESIDENCE AND GREEN-HOUSES.
PHOTO BY CLARK & NOTT.

videre. He is close and careful on estimates and captures many important jobs. Mr. Sturges was born November 9, 1869, in Mt. Morris, N. Y., and came with his parents to Lindenwood, Ogle county, when six months old. He was married February 28, 1894, at Rockford to Miss Anna Wagner. Mr. Sturges is successful in his chosen calling, and his business, especially in the architectural line, is increasing at a gratifying rate.

S. PEPPER,

The North Side florist, came to Belvidere in 1851. In 1862 he enlisted in the service of the United States with Co. "G," 95th Regiment Illinois Volunteers. After participating in many of the notable engagements of the war, he was honorably discharged August 17, 1865, and returned to Belvidere. In 1869 he embarked in the business of floriculture, being the first to make a specialty of this line in Boone county. From small beginnings the facilities were gradually extended, until now his three large greenhouses and extensive hot-bedding plants cover a block, just north of the court house, with the exception of a plot reserved for a handsome new residence. His display of choice roses, plants and palms of every description is at all times complete, and he is in constant readiness to furnish cut flowers and designs for parties, weddings and funerals. That his efforts to adequately serve the public are appreciated is evident from the very large patronage enjoyed.

GROGAN & DENNEY.

This popular firm, composed of J. F. Grogan and J. C. A. Denney, commenced business at the corner of State and Buchanan streets in October, 1893. In

OFFICE OF THE JULIEN HOUSE.
BELVIDERE'S LEADING HOTEL.
PHOTO BY CLARK & SOTT.

1895, finding that the quarters occupied were wholly inadequate to properly house their increasing stock, they removed in August to the present fine location on the west side of the street first named. They deal exclusively in boots, shoes and rubber goods, and carry the most extensive lines in the city. Their specialty is the finer qualities in every width and shape, although commoner grades receive due attention. The shoes carried are made to order by manufacturers whose reputation for the best work and newest styles is established. A short time ago the firm purchased a lot and building a few doors north of the present store. It is the intention to remove the building and erect a fine block, fitted particularly for their business. Mr. Grogan came to Belvidere from Freeport, this state, where he has always resided, and Mr. Denney from Ft. Leavenworth, Kansas. That they understand the requirements of a first-class trade is evident from the character of the stock, its extent and display, and their enviable success as merchants.

C. D. MULFORD.

Mr. Mulford's residence in Belvidere began at a comparatively recent date, that of January 22, 1893. He then opened a large stock of jewelry, watches, clocks and silverware, and is permanently located in a handsome and tastily fitted store on South State street. He was born at Cherry Valley, Ill., October 8, 1870. His people were from New York state, whence so large a portion of the early settlers of this vicinity emigrated. After attendance at the public schools of Rockford, where his education was completed, he mastered every detail in the trade of a watchmaker and jeweler, and considers this the permanent and congenial business of his life. Finishing a three years' sojourn on the Pacific coast, in charge of a leading hot-springs resort at Foley, he returned to Illinois. He was joined in marriage with Miss Ora, daughter of W. F. Allen, at her home in Flora, this county, August 17, 1892. They have one child, a promising boy. A member of the Knights of Pythias he finds fraternal welcome. Mr. Mulford is a gentleman of conservative views, believing that the quieter but dependable methods of business will always win and retain the confidence of the public, and is a type of that valued younger element which is infusing life and energy into the commercial and social circles of this progressive city.

MISS L. MAE BLOSSOM,

Proprietor of an extensive millinery establishment on South State street, first turned her attention to this especially creative art early in life. Becoming an adept, she left her home in Rockford, and opened rooms at Morrison, this state, and, after remaining there for a time, came to Belvidere about three years ago, where she has since been engaged in business. The large stock, manufactured and in material, now carried indicates rare taste and care in selection, and was bought, as are all the purchases made, from only leading and reliable houses. Her productions are pronounced by those competent of judging to be not merely copies but distinctive styles adapted to individual requirements. With the particular object of furnishing the newest fashions as the seasons come, and employing none but skilled assistants, her very marked success is amply accounted for.

UNITY BUILDING.

The splendid structure illustrated on next page, and located on North State street, was erected in 1895 by Messrs. Witbeck & Kellogg. It is not surpassed in design or exceeded in expense by any other in the city, and excels in solidity and thoroughness of construction. The interior is arranged for stores, offices and flats, with light basements. The finish and appointments are of the finest and most modern description, and the building is one of the notable adornments of Belvidere's business streets.

John L. Witbeck, one of the joint owners, although now residing in the city, is still engaged in farming on an extensive scale. He was born in Athens, N. Y., February 19, 1842. Mr. Witbeck was married to Miss Marietta Olney, of Belvidere in 1864. They have five children, May, Olney, Alice, Ethel and Isaac T. Shortly after his marriage he assumed the management of the property, his father removing to Belvidere. Land was added and improvements made, and this 320 acres is now one of the most valuable farms in the county. In 1892 he occupied the homestead in Belvidere, his father having died some years ago. Mr. Witbeck's time is largely taken up with other financial interests, and he is a director in the First and Second National banks.

John L. Kellogg, his associate, was born in Iowa, and is forty-five years of age. For the past ten years he has been a resident of Belvidere, but in the fall of last year removed with his family to Rumsey, California, where a fine fruit farm was awaiting their occupancy. He was married at Sycamore, this state, to a daughter of L. P. Wood. Mr. Kellogg is a veteran railroad conductor, having been engaged in that service for over twenty-five years, his last connection being for a long period with the Chicago and Northwestern.

THE UNITY BLOCK.
PHOTO BY CLARK & NOTT.

F. W. STARR.

Two years' experience in the hardware line has convinced F. W. Starr that he is at last fitted into the right niche. Perhaps the reason why he is so confident is that he has had two years of great prosperity, the past one having been phenomenally so. He has sold tons of stoves, and put in no less than sixteen Prince Royal furnaces, certainly an enviable record for a new establishment. For eleven years he was in the wholesale and retail oil business. Mr. Starr foresaw the future growth of Belvidere in time to make a small fortune in the real estate business. Some years ago before the city began its remarkable growth he platted Hinsdell & Starr's addition and resurvey, F. W. Starr's subdivision and second subdivision, all in the southwest part of town. Here he has already disposed of between 300 and 400 lots, but still has left some of the best for building purposes.

Although Mr. Starr is a native of Forreston, Ill., he has resided in Belvidere since infancy. He is a prominent member of the Methodist Episcopal church, being one of its official board.

W. W. BRITTAN.

"Always at the Front" is the motto of W. W. Brittan, whose bakery goods are known in nearly every home in Belvidere. Mr. Brittan has been in the bakery trade in Belvidere for over seven years. Each year his business increases, proving

SOUTH STATE STREET, LOOKING SOUTH IN BUSINESS SECTION.

the popularity of his goods. Two delivery wagons are run around the city and it keeps them busy to cover the routes. Mr. Brittan recently purchased a lot on North State street and will build a fine bakery establishment. In connection with his bakery he conducts a restaurant and confectionery, and commands a large patronage. He is enterprising and progressive and has scores of friends. In short, he is one of the most successful young business men of Belvidere.

WILLIAM M. SAWYER.

The term "jewelry" is rather comprehensive when applied to the general stock of to-day. So great is the variety of articles combining artistic form with practical value, that the designation covers many departments. At a central location on South State street William M. Sawyer conducts one of the most successful enterprises of this kind in the city. The stock carried has been selected with great care and includes everything desirable in watches, clocks, silverware, optical goods, art wares and kindred lines. Watch repairing, always a leading feature of the retail business, is given especial attention, while the rule in regard to prices is to place them at the lowest point consistent with good value. Mr. Sawyer is a son of James W. and Ruie D. Sawyer, and was born in St. Louis,

Mo., October 6, 1869. His father came with his parents to Cook county, this state, in 1836, from Stockbridge, Vt. In 1860 he went to Wisconsin, and at the breaking out of the war enlisted in the First Wisconsin battery. On his discharge he located at St. Louis, remaining there until 1870, when he came to Belvidere and embarked in the lumber business. In 1876 he was elected circuit clerk of this county, and reëlected in 1880, but died in 1884, a short time prior to the expiration of his term. Mr. Sawyer will be remembered as an exceptionally capable and popular official. The subject of this sketch has been in business for himself only four years, but in that time has built up a trade which compares favorably with that of older houses, and is constantly increasing. He was mar-

WM. M. SAWYER.
PHOTO BY CLARK & NOTT.

ried to Miss Linnie Macdonald, of Belvidere, October 2, 1893. They have one son, James Donald, born March 30, 1896. Mr. Sawyer is fraternally connected with the Sons of Veterans and Royal Arcanum.

SENNEFF & PILE.

The addition to the merchants of Belvidere of such an enterprising firm as Senneff & Pile gives us a confectionery, fruit and cigar store which would do credit to a city five times as large. Less than a year ago this firm moved here from Chicago. Their place is fitted up in elegant fashion, the fixtures alone costing a small fortune. The soda fountain is a magnificent adornment. Senneff & Pile handle a line of fancy candies of their own make that few stores can equal. They also handle one of the largest lines of choice cigars in town. In fact they run their business in Chicago style, and the people point with pride to their store. Besides manufacturing fancy candies for the wholesale as well as the retail trade they make ice cream of the most delicious kind. The firm has a store in Dixon, Ill., and both are run in metropolitan style. Mr. Pile has charge of the Belvidere store, and although not one of the old business men of the city, he has already established himself firmly in business Belvidere. He is an expert candymaker, and it will not be long before Belvidere candy will be known all over this section.

REICHERT BROS.

At the corner of State street and Logan avenue is one of the most complete hardware establishments in the city. The proprietors, Reichert Brothers, came here about two years ago from the east, and have demonstrated that they know how to conduct a first-class hardware store. The members of the firm are H. H. and Chas. T. Reichert, both of whom have had ample experience in this line.

F. S. PIEL.

F. S. PIEL.

At the corner of North State street and Lincoln avenue is a popular grocery establishment whose proprietor is F. S. Piel. Mr. Piel was born and reared in Belvidere, and therefore has a wide acquaintance. His father, Richard Piel, was one of the oldest settlers. Eight years ago he embarked in the line of business since followed, and his trade has kept pace with the growth of the city. Long experience, good judgment in purchasing and fair dealing, have attracted a desirable and extended list of customers. Mr. Piel's confidence in the future of Belvidere is manifested in the constant increase of stock. His business and social standing is high, and he is to be numbered among the younger and enterprising merchants who have been the principal factors in the city's later advancement.

MOSES LUCAS

Is one of the reliable and well-known citizens of Belvidere, whose acquaintance, from long residence and frequent contact with the people, is coextensive with the limits of the county. He was born in Flora, this county, June 1, 1851. He was a son of Horace and Elizabeth Lucas, who came from the East to Boone county in 1836, this date marking them as among the earliest pioneers, and settled on a farm in Flora. An elder brother was the second child born in this county, one other ranking him but two or three months. In 1869 Mr. Lucas left the farm and cast his lot with the people of Belvidere. He engaged with E. W. Case the grocery dealer as clerk, and remained with him for a consecutive period of fourteen years. Upon terminating this connection he followed the avocation of farming for some years, but finally began business for himself in feed and grain, and is now located on South State street. Mr. Lucas was married to Miss Nettie Lane of this city. They have one son, Bert R., now in the employ of the *Northwestern*. The elegant new home on Pearl street has recently been completed and occupied by the family.

WILBUR HAMMOND,
BELVIDERE'S SPIRITUALISTIC HEALER.

HAMMOND, THE HEALER.

Belvidere has been widely advertised by Wilbur Hammond, the healer, whose marvelous cures have astonished all who have heard of them. Many refuse to believe that Hammond can heal by his magnetic touch, but the recorded cases of cure stand as evidence. Hammond was born north of the city on a farm. He has always taken a deep interest in spiritualistic matters. Not until about a year ago did he discover his power of healing. He goes into a trance and claims to be controlled by a deceased German physician. Patients from far and near flock to Belvidere to be "treated" by the healer.

A. SCHERRER,

Manager of the Scherrer Tailoring Company, one of the leading outfitting establishments of the city, was born at Williamsburg, N. Y., in 1856. Subsequent to a trial of various locations he came to Belvidere, about eleven years ago, and for several years had charge of J. M. Glasner's tailoring department. His present quarters are on North State street, in the Opera House block, where, with fine assortment of foreign and domestic woolens and the most competent workmen, he caters to those inclined to obtain the best in ordered garments at reasonable prices. Mr. Scherrer is a charter member of Boone Camp 51, M. W. A., and commander of Kishwaukee Tent 61, K. O. T. M. He is also one of the trustees of the First Presbyterian church, of which he is an active member. He was married to Miss Ellen Fraher in 1880, at Clyde, New York state. They have two promising children, a daughter and son.

JONES AND WINNIE.

This enterprising firm is among the newer additions to the commercial interests of Belvidere. Opening last fall a complete stock of groceries in the Longcor block, on North State street, it attracted by the extent and variety of the display a large patronage which increases as time familiarizes the public with its methods of transacting business. While the lines include everything required by the

A. SCHERRER.
PHOTO BY CLARK & NOTT.

patrons of a first-class grocery establishment, a special effort is made to furnish the finest grades of tea and coffee, together with medium selections, at moderate prices. The staple of flour, sometimes difficult to obtain in desirable brands, is purchased from the most reliable mills and guaranteed the very best on the market. Spices, canned goods and fruits in their season receive particular attention, and are always first in quality. The senior partner, Mr. S. J. Jones, was formerly in the same trade here, but a number of years since went to Dakota, where he engaged in farming, some time ago returning to Belvidere. His experience for many years in the line again taken up, will be mutually valuable to himself and the customers of the house. He was a soldier in the late war, and is a member of Hurlbut Post G. A. R., this city. Mr. A. Winnie, his business associate, comes from New York state, and has every qualification requisite in an enterprise of this nature. The purpose of the firm is to win the confidence of the community in the reliability of the products they offer, their good faith in dealing with customers, and disposition to be abreast of the times in character of stock and a low range of prices.

CHARLES E. KELSEY.

Mr. Kelsey is one of the veteran publishers and music dealers of Belvidere. Born in Clinton, Conn., in 1834, and in early years developing a talent for musical interpretation, he was, at the age of eighteen, appointed organist of the church in his native town. From that time until about six years ago he has served various organizations in this capacity. First visiting Belvidere in 1858, he shortly afterward returned, and was united in marriage to Miss Ellen E. Tomkins. She was a daughter of Enos Tomkins, one of the early and prominent citizens of Belvidere, now deceased. The first stock of parlor organs brought into this county was consigned to Mr. Kelsey. In 1878 he founded, with Rev. W. A. Welsher, the semi-weekly *Recorder*. Later, Mr. Kelsey purchased Mr. Welsher's interest, and afterward took as partner Charles A. Church. The new firm continued the publication for several years, when the senior partner retired, and opened an office for commercial printing. Last year he formed a partnership with Prof. Mark M. Jones, of Chicago—a gentleman with thirty-five years' experience as teacher, composer, and dealer—and a line of pianos and organs was added to the printing department. Mr. Kelsey is an inventor as well as practical printer, and a few years ago brought to perfection a process, originating with himself, for printing thirty separate colors at one impression. He is a high Mason, and has served the local organization in an official capacity for many years. Genial, energetic and patriotic—with special reference to progressive Belvidere—Mr. Kelsey reaps the reward of continuous faith and effort in the confidence of the public and regard of a wide acquaintance.

C. E. KELSEY.
PHOTO BY YOUNGT.

NEW YORK CONDENSING CO.

The New York Milk Condensing Company established a branch in Belvidere over a year ago, and fifty men are now employed at the factory. The company built a plant costing about $75,000, it being one of the finest in the west. It has proved a boon to the farmers who never before got such prices for their milk. J. H. Southard is local manager and has made many warm friends since coming to Belvidere. He is thoroughly competent for the work, and has the confidence of all with whom he has business transactions.

THE DAILY REPUBLICAN.

The Daily Republican prides itself on being one of the most successful country dailies in the state. The paper is an eight column folio and is liberally patronized by the people of Belvidere. Three years ago A. H. Keeler and Frank T. Moran launched the first successful daily ever published in Belvidere. Mr. Moran retired from the firm nine months later, and after a year's work in Rockford journalism returned to Belvidere and purchased a half interest in the *Boone County Republican*, then published by Chas. Beverly. The new firm bought the daily of Mr. Keeler and conducted it until January 1, 1896, when Mr. Moran became sole proprietor. The weekly edition run in connection with the daily has a large and increasing circulation.

THE DAILY REPUBLICAN OFFICE AND EMPLOYES.
PHOTO BY CLARK & NOTT.

The editor of The Republican, though young in years, has had over seven years' experience in the journalistic field. Born near Rockford twenty-four years ago he attended the public schools, and subsequently entered Rockford Academy, from which institution he graduated. He taught school for a time in Winnebago county, and then took up newspaper work. He was engaged six years in Rockford, rising from a reportorial position on the *Morning Republican* to city editor. On April 3, 1894, he married Miss Edna Galey, of Rockford.

A. F. Conklin, late city editor of the Rockford *Morning Republican*, holds a similar position with the Belvidere Republican. He is a clever writer and good all-round newspaper man. C. H. Seiders, whose experience in newspaper work dates back eighteen years, is advertising manager, and is well equipped for the work. M. L. Marshall is foreman of the job rooms and Ezra Merrill foreman of the composing force.

This creditable production, "Belvidere Illustrated," speaks louder for the enterprise of the paper than complimentary words.

FRANK T. MORAN.

A. F. CONKLIN,
CITY EDITOR THE REPUBLICAN.

JACK EDWARDS,
A CLEVER AND PROMISING SKETCH ARTIST.

CHAS. H. SEIDERS,
ADVERTISING MANAGER THE REPUBLICAN.

GEN'L A. C. FULLER, President.　　　　　　　D. D. SABIN, Vice-President.
IRVING TERWILLIGER, Cashier.　　　　　　　FRANK SEWELL, Ass't Cashier.

SECOND NATIONAL BANK,
BELVIDERE, ILL.

Capital, $100,000　　　　　　Undivided Profits, $32,000

Interest Allowed on Certificates of Deposit.

DIRECTORS.

ALLEN C. FULLER,　　D. D. SABIN,　　MARK RAMSEY,　　W. F. HOVEY,
　　IRVING TERWILLIGER,　　W. S. DUNTON,　　J. L. WITBECK.

WM. D. SWAIL, President.　　　　　　　　F. S. WHITMAN, Vice-Pres't.
JOHN GREENLEE, Cashier.　　　　　　　　B. F. HARNISH, Ass't Cashier.

Organized under the General Banking Law of the State of Illinois,
Sept., 1889.

THE PEOPLE'S BANK OF BELVIDERE,
BELVIDERE, ILLINOIS.

Paid-Up Capital, $50,000.00
Surplus and Undivided Profits, $20,000.00

A GENERAL BANKING BUSINESS TRANSACTED.

Prompt Attention given to Collections.　　　Foreign Exchange Bought and Sold.
　　　　　　　　　Correspondence Solicited.

MARK RAMSEY, President.　　　　　　　ALBERT E. LOOP, Cashier.
WM. S. DUNTON, Vice-President.　　　　　CHARLES D. LOOP, Teller.

ESTABLISHED IN 1865.

FIRST NATIONAL BANK
OF BELVIDERE, ILL.

Capital, $75,000.00　　　　　　Surplus, $21,000.00

Interest Allowed on Certificates of Deposit.

DIRECTORS.

JOHN J. FOOTE,　　HENRY W. AVERY,　　JOHN L. WITBECK,　　WM. S. DUNTON,
　　JOHN M. GLASNER,　　IRVING TERWILLIGER,　　ALBERT E. LOOP,
　　　　　　　　　MARK RAMSEY.

www.ingramcontent.com/pod-product-compliance
Lightning Source LLC
Chambersburg PA
CBHW020302170426
43202CB00008B/475